WHAT PEOPLE ARE SAYING ABOUT
Selling to the C-Suite

"The business world is drowning in a flood of sales books. The trouble is that most of these books are about how to sell, without a clue about how customers buy, and so they do more harm than good. This book is different. It is firmly rooted in how people buy, and so it works. And an added bonus that particularly appeals to me: the book is based on research, which makes it rare and welcome."

—Neil Rackham, author of *SPIN Selling*
and seminal thinker on sales effectiveness

"As an educator on the college level teaching professional selling, I found this book to be invaluable if you are interested in learning how to sell to the top executives. Not only does it help you understand when to engage the executive, it also tells you how to get access. If that was not enough, the book also focuses on how to create value and build credibility with the executives. It is a must read for anyone who interacts with top executives."

—Dan C. Weilbaker, Ph.D., McKesson Pharmaceutical Group
Professor of Sales, Northern Illinois University

"This book is like a one-day MBA in Selling to Executives. A must read for sales professionals—both new and experienced—who want to get better at their craft."

—Tom Martin, President, Strategy 2 Revenue, and former
President of North America, Miller Heiman, Inc.

"Sales professionals who align with key executive decision makers early in the sales process have a higher win rate and make more money than their peers. Steve and Nic have meticulously researched and distilled the best practices that distinguish the salespeople who can sell at the executive level and are seen as Trusted Advisors. Credibility is the foundation of being a Trusted Advisor. *Selling to the C-Suite* lays out when and how to access executives, as well as how to establish credibility and value."

—Bill Walden, former Director of Sales Effectiveness, The TAS Group

"If Sun Tzu lived today, he would write this book. Chinese executives seek relationships to help their personal agenda and reduce their risk. *Selling to the C-Suite* is full of sage advice from two master practitioners on how to become a 'relationship master,' but most importantly, it is based on the executive's view. We were honored to partner in China on the research project, and this book brings those secrets to life in exciting ways."

—Anne An 安欣, Chief Learning Officer,
hi-Soft Technology International, and former manager of the
Hewlett-Packard Business School, Beijing, China

"A straightforward, pragmatic approach on how to gain and retain access to the executive level. Those new to executive sales will find a game plan they can use immediately. Veterans who regularly call on executives will use this book to sharpen their game."

—Chip Brubaker, Vice President, Americas
Sales Readiness, Computer Associates

"Too many salespeople have no idea if they're winning or losing, and it's usually because they're meeting the wrong people and asking the wrong questions too low down the food chain. As a result, their sales forecasts are no better than a lottery. This book pulls no punches in showing why sales and marketing fails to connect to executives, and what to do about it."

—Gordon Clubb, Managing Director, SAS Institute
Australia & New Zealand

"I finished this book in one sitting; it is easy to read, and I was very impressed. It holds practical advice on how to get to the decision makers in the context of sales, but also applies in many other situations where the objective is influence. Having learned these lessons the hard way while transforming a Chinese state-owned enterprise into a globally competitive business, I wish this book had been available when I first started!"

—Geoff Watson, Vice President, Alcoa China

"Nic Read and Dr. Bistritz show us how to reach out to executives using ideas from those executives. It's proven, and it works."

—Andy Sim, Director, Commercial Business,
Singapore, Cisco Systems

"We hear a lot about being a Trusted Advisor, but what does that really mean? The authors clearly define that role with the insight, definition, and actions required to establish and sustain credible value-based engagements with senior executives. If your success depends on being engaged early in your customer's decision process and you're in a market that demands value-based differentiation, then this is a must read."

—Gary Summy, Direct Sales Development,
Trane Commercial Systems, and Director of the Strategic
Account Management Association (SAMA)

"Nothing on your shelf right now will tell you more about why salespeople fail to engage with CXOs, or what they need to do to earn the role of Trusted Advisor. Supported by revealing research and cutting insights, Read and Bistritz take you on a journey to discover why salespeople fail to engage with CXOs, and provide practical advice on what they need to do to earn their way in."

—Hugh Macfarlane, author of *The Leaky Funnel*
and CEO of MathMarketing

"This book offers something for every salesperson no matter how long they've been selling. For the new entrant to the profession, it offers proven tips for getting to the executive suite. For the seasoned salesperson, it provides time-honored techniques for staying there!"

"To not adopt these concepts puts you at risk of being left out in the lobby, while your competitor is in the client's boardroom."

"Finally, a book on selling to executives that isn't built on yesterday's traditional sales thinking! Anyone who's serious about the business of selling—as it exists today—needs to read this book."

"This book clearly explains the nature of different relationships within an organization and is a great guide to navigating your way through them to increase your prospect of making a sale. In my experience, the depth and breadth of your relationship as a Trusted Advisor best ensures your selling success. I also particularly liked the comment that marketing executives need to understand that marketing should be about making money."

"Most of what's out there from the experts on selling to executives is as dated as the cassette tapes we heard their message on the first time! *Selling to the C-Suite* offers a fresh, Internet-age view on why selling at the top matters so much in today's global B2B sales environment. The authors shed new light on the realities that make selling to executives harder to do today than ever before, and offer street-level coaching on how to secure ongoing executive access to drive unrivaled leverage!"

"This book is absolutely *on the button* in terms of relevance to any sales organization, as it dispels so many myths and reinvigorates a sales team's attention to the real art of selling. Sales staff at all levels should keep this by their bed or on their desk, and refer to it daily!"
—Andrew Moon, CEO, Billback Systems

"The book puts into words what successful sales reps practice—mostly unaware of doing so. As a salesman and trainer, I love how it is able to generate a *that's it! moment* for both battle-hardened and new reps, especially summarized points that they can quickly act on."
—Ian Loh, Director, Sales Productivity, EMC South Asia

"If you've always wondered how the other sales guy got to the CEO and you didn't, start reading this book and earn serious commissions!"
—Lindsay Lyon, Founder and Chairman, Datacatch Inc., and former General Manager, Commercial Sales, Hewlett-Packard Australia

"If ever there were insights into the minds of today's executives, this book is it. Based on solid research, Steve Bistritz and Nic Read share with you what today's executives are thinking, how to get in front of them, and what to do when you get there. The appendixes alone should be a mandatory read for any high-level sales representative."
—Gary Connor, author of *Sales: Games and Activities for Trainers*

"How quickly we fall into a comfort zone of selling features and benefits, but in most cases this just won't cut it at the executive level. In a world where the marketing and sales functions are being reshaped by the impact of the Internet, this book provides timely guidance, backed up by research into what drives decision makers at the top. After reading this book, you will find yourself taking lessons from it straight to your next prospect meeting—and it works!"
—Bill McNamara, CEO, Marketing Decisions, Eloqua distributor

"This is a very practical approach to calling on executives. The authors tell us why it is important and how to do it. Getting access to the executive level is one battle, but knowing what to talk to them about when you get there is another. This book provides a road map. Every organization calling on Fortune 1000 companies needs this information."

—Renie McClay, former president of the Professional Society for Sales and Marketing Training (SMT)

"In today's selling environment, having the confidence and the knowledge to sell at the C-level is often the difference between success and failure for B2B sales teams. In a clear, concise, and compelling way, Steve Bistritz and Nic Read solve the mysteries surrounding selling to senior executives and provide all the tools and resources needed to access, leverage, and create winning relationships in the corner office. Definitely a must read."

—Chris Deren, CEO, Sellmasters

"Great information on a critical topic for all salespeople. The sale to an executive is made during the questioning process, not in your product presentation. You can't sell anything to an executive until you have first sold yourself."

—Duane Sparks, author of *Action Selling* and Chairman, The Sales Board

"More and more sales organizations are realizing that the most effective means to *get ink* is to start at the top of the management chain and work your way down to exactly the right office. The trouble is, many sales professionals are skittish about making contact with anyone in a position greater than middle management for fear of being rejected. *Selling to the C-Suite* is a no-nonsense road map for sales pros who are ready to try something highly effective. Steve and Nic have put together a powerful guide that will soon have you aiming for the executive suite with confidence."

—Dan Walker, Executive Producer, SalesRepRadio.com

"The data is real, the suggestions are right on target, and the tools are designed to help any sales professional succeed in selling to the CXO level. Identifying the relevant executive and becoming a trusted business advisor take dedication and determination. This book has outlined all the necessary steps to guide you for several years to come. I'm buying a copy for each member of my sales organization, and I'd recommend this book to anyone who wants to be the best in their field."

—Vince Melograna, formerly National Sales Director, Base-Line, Inc.

"Bistritz and Read are world-class experts in the discipline of selling to executives. Savvy sales professionals, as well as the senior executives they report to, will value *Selling to the C-Suite* as *the* guide to gaining and maintaining access to those most-influential members of the customer's executive team—the inner circle."

—David Stein, CEO and Founder, ES Research Group, Inc.

"In the current changing market, we all need to show our unique value to customers. To help them become true Trusted Advisors, all of our salespeople will learn from this book."

—Atsuhiro Ozeki, General Manager, Fuji Xerox
Learning Institute Inc., Tokyo, Japan

"Being capable of selling at the executive level is more essential now than ever before. Those who can communicate value and build a relationship of trust with senior executives become the real stars in today's sales universe. This book can be your rocket to success."

—Charles Bates, CEO, WinningByDesign

"Very insightful and practical. I can see this book being invaluable to all sales professionals, especially those who focus on the B2B arena. Plus it's written in plain English with good examples that help explain the intricacies, theories, and art of selling."

—Kevin Fong, CEO, China Automobile Association, a subsidiary of IAG

"Nic Read and Dr. Bistritz have done a masterful job summarizing how to approach and sell to executives. If you read this and apply its secrets, you'll win more, more of the time."
—Michael Gallagher, President, The Stevie Awards for Sales & Customer Service

"*Selling to the C-Suite* is the ultimate resource for those who want to get through to the most powerful decision makers in today's business world. Globalization is happening now, and Nic Read and Dr. Bistritz have the experience, the know-how, and the research to guide you."
—Dan Hill, President, Sensory Logic, Inc., and author of *Emotionomics: Winning Hearts and Minds*

"Based on real research and great insights into how and why executives buy, Steve and Nic provide a pathway to success for anyone selling at the executive level. It doesn't matter where you are in your sales career, you will benefit from this book."
—Paul Aldo, Ph.D., President, Executive Performance Solutions, Inc.

"Steve and Nic provide a great history lesson that helps us understand why marketing and sales is different in the new millennium and provides the research background to prove their points. If you want to become effective at the C-suite, this book and its references, models, and tools are incredible."
—Jim Graham, former Chief Learning Officer, R.R. Donnelley

SELLING
TO THE
C-SUITE

SELLING
TO THE
C-SUITE

WHAT EVERY EXECUTIVE
WANTS YOU TO KNOW
ABOUT SUCCESSFULLY
SELLING TO THE TOP

NICHOLAS A.C. READ
STEPHEN J. BISTRITZ, Ed.D.

New York   Chicago   San Francisco   Lisbon   London
Madrid   Mexico City   Milan   New Delhi   San Juan
Seoul   Singapore   Sydney   Toronto

The McGraw·Hill Companies

4 5 6 7 8 9 0   DOC/DOC   1 5 4 3 2 1

ISBN 978-0-07-162891-4
MHID 0-07-162891-6

McGraw-Hill books are available at special quantity discounts to use as premiums and sales promotions, or for use in corporate training programs. To contact a representative, please e-mail us at bulksales@mcgraw-hill.com.

This book is printed on acid-free paper.

Library of Congress Cataloging-in-Publication Data
Read, Nicholas A.C.
    Selling to the C-suite : what every executive wants you to know about successfully selling to the top / by Nicholas A.C. Read and Stephen J. Bistritz.
        p. cm.
    ISBN 0-07-162891-6 (alk. paper)
    1. Selling. 2. Sales executives. I. Bistritz, Stephen J. II. Title.
    HF5438.25.R38   2010
    658.85–dc22

                                                2009011076

Contents

CONTENTS

Foreword

Neil Rackham

Sales has grown up a lot in the last 10 years, and this book is a good example of just how far selling has come. When the manuscript first landed on my desk, I looked at the title, *Selling to the C-Suite,* and I couldn't suppress a groan. "Another collection of impractical advice about how to get in front of any key executive without even trying," I thought. And you can't blame me for being skeptical. Almost without exception, books on how to get access to "The Man," "VITO," "the fox," or a dozen other names for the top dog whose signature can change your life, have been mediocre and unrealistic. So, I must admit, I started reading with very low expectations.

By the time I reached the end of the first chapter, all that had changed. Three things were immediately evident:

- There is a refreshing realism about the authors' advice. No gimmicks, no tricks, no smoke and mirrors. Selling successfully at C-level is hard, thoughtful, and strategic, and the book offers none of the usual unrealistic silver bullets.

- The ideas are based on research, not on anecdotes. The authors interviewed hundreds of senior executives to learn about their buying practices and, for this alone, the book is worth its weight in commission checks.
- It is one of the few books that actually demonstrates an understanding of selling in a global business environment. There are cases and examples from—among other places—China, Europe, and Australia. Everybody says we must think globally. Nic Read and Stephen Bistritz have been doing it. They have been working all over the world, and they really understand global business because they live it every day.

Selling to the C-Suite comes at the right moment. Nic Read and Stephen Bistritz have been developing this material for 10 years, and they couldn't have timed their publication better. There are three intersecting factors that put the book at the center of a perfect storm that is changing selling in fundamental ways.

THE ECONOMY IN CRISIS

These are unprecedented times when even the super-confident economic gurus readily confess that they don't know what's going on or how long it will be before that comforting word "normal" can be safely used again. Prediction is rapidly going out of style. Yet I'll venture one confident prediction based on the history of every economic downturn for the past century. When the economy goes down, the decisions go up. A purchasing decision that is made in good times at a middle management level requires active participation from the top when company survival is at stake. Selling cycles take longer, and customers become risk averse. In this environment, the ability to sell effectively at C-level has never been so important. The advice in this book can make all the difference. Here's just one example. From their research, Read and Bistritz identify where in the sales cycle C-level executives get involved, why they get involved, and what this means for an effective sales strategy. Very few of the salespeople I work with understand the dynamics of top management involvement, and this book will certainly help them.

THE NEW CEO ROLE

In the good old days, CEOs could succeed by looking for improvement inside the company. By cutting away fat and by introducing systems, processes, TQM, and the like, their organizations became lean, mean, and competitive. Today, with a few endangered exceptions in the much vilified financial and pharmaceutical industries, the fat is gone, and the company runs like clockwork. So how does a CEO make an impact? The fashionable answer has been acquisition. Grow the company by buying your competition. But, in today's environment, raising the capital for acquisition has become next to impossible. What's more, the track record of acquisitions has proved spotty and questionable. With the traditional growth strategies unavailable or discredited, CEOs are now turning outward. The new role of the CEO is to create value at the organization's boundaries, to radically change relationships with suppliers, customers, and alliance partners. This creates significant opportunities for the few salespeople who can relate at an enterprise level with their customers. The authors worked closely with Hewlett-Packard and saw, firsthand, how the top hundred HP accounts brought in upwards of $13 billion in 2005. To generate this kind of revenue, the account executives for each of these accounts not only had to work at C-level in order to understand the customer's strategies and politics but they also had to use extraordinary creativity to help their customers find new value from their collaboration. I detect much of their experience in the pages of *Selling to the C-Suite*.

THE VALUE CREATION IMPERATIVE

The final factor that makes this such a timely book is a trend that has been gathering pace for several years. The old role of sales—to show customers why your products and services are better than those of your competitors—is no longer viable. It's too expensive, and customers don't want it. Salespeople who still cling to this traditional role (I call them "talking brochures," while the authors here use the curiously similar term "walking brochures"— take your pick) are failing everywhere. In their place, the new salespeople are highly skilled value creators, who live by ingeniously solving customer problems. The measure of these new salespeople is the value they create and, to create maximum value, they must understand the issues and concerns of their C-suite customers. This book is timely and essential reading for them.

Neil Rackham
Author of *SPIN Selling*
Visiting Professor of Sales and Marketing,
Portsmouth Business School
Visiting Professor of Sales Strategy,
Cranfield University

Preface

If you've ever tried and failed to meet a senior executive that you needed to sell to, this book is for you. If you've managed to nail a first meeting at the C-level, but the executive later froze you out, you'll learn what went wrong and how to solve it. And even if you've already mastered the executive call, don't relax just yet; the rise of globalized, nontraditional hierarchies and borderless organizations means that you may have mastered a set of skills for a world that no longer exists!

You owe it to yourself, to your employer, and, most important, to your clients to read, ponder, and apply the golden nuggets waiting to be discovered here. It's not the first book written on this topic, but it *is* the most relevant for today's global market, no matter whether you sell in Mumbai, Manchester, Melbourne, or Manhattan!

That's a pretty tall claim. Can we back it up? Like any salespeople worth their salt, we give three solid validations:

1. *We've written this book from a combined 60 years of experience selling on corporate front lines around the world.* From IT, communications, and professional services to banking, insurance,

and manufacturing, between us we've carried a bag, beat the street, and walked the talk for a variety of large-ticket business-to-business solutions for more than five decades—and not just in one culture, but in many countries across Europe, the Middle East and Africa, Asia-Pacific, North America, and Latin America. We have enough war stories and frequent-flyer miles to know what we're talking about.

2. *This book is based on empirical research.* We couldn't find any books written on this topic that held anything more than personal anecdotes of what the author did in her glory days. While trips down Memory Lane may have some value, they tell you only the *salesperson's opinion* about how executives buy. We wanted to dig deeper and get inside the heads of living, breathing executives to see what's really going on in there during the decision-making process.

So we commissioned groundbreaking research of our own, and we jumped onto any other project team we could find where executive buying habits were the focus of study, particularly those run by Hewlett-Packard in North America; the Hewlett-Packard Business School in Beijing, China; Target Marketing Systems; the Kenan-Flagler School of Business at the University of North Carolina; and the Center for Business & Industrial Marketing at Georgia State University.

After delving into the executive brain for 10 years, we're ready to share with you what C-suite leaders in 500 diverse companies and government bodies told us (purchasing and middle managers were excluded) in response to interviews that asked probing questions such as:

- *When do executives get involved in the buying process for major decisions?*
- *How do salespeople gain access to executives?*
- *How can salespeople establish credibility with executives?*
- *How can salespeople create value at the executive level?*

- *Is executive buying behavior consistent across cultures?*
  As you do more of the things that senior executives respond to, you'll command greater credibility, close more business, and make more money.
3. *Thousands of sales professionals have already field-tested these concepts.* We decided that the best way to test our research was to turn it into a training workshop and have salespeople around the world put it over a Bunsen burner. We carefully noted their feedback to isolate a distillation of best practices. That's what this book is all about. More on this revolutionary workshop can be found at www.sellxl.com.

We continue to receive e-mails from students about epic struggles that they fought and won against fierce competitors because they were able to get onto the executive's radar and raise the bar. We've selected two quick examples from opposite corners of the world to illustrate.

Karen, an account manager for a telecommunications carrier in Australia, told us:

My major account was about to turn to a competitor. I'd tried everything to appease the client, but the contracts manager had found a better price from a smaller carrier, and in truth, as the big gorilla, we'd been arrogant in expecting that this client would never change suppliers. I was about to lose this large flagship account when I was sent to your training. I applied what I learned and was able to gain immediate access above the contracts manager to the senior executive who would be most affected by a change of supplier. Your process ran like clockwork. I knew where I needed to steer the discussion and what to say, and this executive responded exactly as I hoped he would. The bottom line is that I saved the account, and I learned a valuable lesson about staying aligned with my customers. Several months later, the relationship is at an all-time high. I have no doubt that this is a direct result of what I learned from your research and your workshop.

Conny, a top account manager for a data warehousing vendor in Germany, shares this story:

> I was selling to the IT managers in a major finance and insurance company. Their project had a budget of 200,000 euro with a decision date 12 months away. After learning in your training how to become a business advisor to executives, I was able to rise above the operations level and find a middle-level sponsor who took me to the CEO. When I positioned my pitch around business outcomes instead of technology, my competitors were like ants at my feet. The CEO had wider issues than the IT manager knew about, more budget, and the ability to make the decision after just a few meetings. My sale expanded to 800,000 euro, and I closed it within 6 months—higher and faster than I could ever have achieved without executive alignment.

Interesting isn't it? Salespeople like these were already experienced, they had sales managers whose job it was to coach them, and they had already attended their company's sales induction and other training. And yet they still lacked the knowledge to excel with executives.

Why?

It's our observation that most traditional wisdom about selling to executives is actually at odds with what executives themselves tell us works. And that's a massive problem with the sales profession today. It's as if the last 40 years of corporate sales training have been based more on anecdotes and folklore than on any real science. So when we hear sales managers and trainers teach generalities like "always sell at the top," frankly, we cringe. In a simpler time, when the guy running a business was the guy who owned the business (what we now call small to medium enterprises, or SME), chances are that calling on the "very important top officer" would put you in the ballpark. But today's large companies can represent a labyrinth of global business units where politics, external advisors, and delegated authority affect the decision-making process in ways that were never considered by the collective wisdom of several decades ago.

Today, blindly calling on a senior executive *just because he's a senior executive* will do more harm than good. What if this executive has no skin in the game on this decision? What if it's a project that will never rise to his pay grade? What if he's already handed the project down to a competent subordinate and doesn't see the need to remain involved? What if he's too new in his role to have any political clout? What if he's about to retire and is merely a figurehead in the exit lounge or assigned to only the most insignificant special projects? What if he's recently made a few bad decisions, and any vendor he now sponsors will be tarred with the same brush?

It can cost you the deal if the guy at the top isn't the *relevant executive*. This relevant executive is the one who most feels the pain, most owns the problem you can solve, and will most richly reward you for providing a solution. The relevant executive will be someone with a combination of rank and political influence, with an internal network that allows her to initiate projects, kill projects, intervene in projects, and find funding, both in her own silo and across departmental boundaries. What the relevant executive wants, she gets. And the relevant executive isn't always found at the C-level. This is why "always sell at the top" can be your fastest ticket out of the race.

What's missing from the toolkits of today's road warriors is a set of simple approaches for identifying the relevant executive, enlisting the support of gatekeepers, getting past the roadblocks, creating interest when you land the first meeting, and continuing to add value so that you establish credibility as a business resource.

Case in point: in a recent meeting with the chief information officer of a Fortune 500 technology company, we asked, "Why would someone at your level ever agree to spend time with a salesperson?" The CIO's answer was simple:

> In my experience, professional salespeople offer me suggestions about solutions to business problems that even people in my own organization can't solve. Some of these salespeople have encountered similar problems in other organizations and have creatively addressed them. That's what I expect from salespeople who want to have a Trusted Advisor relationship with me.

In this simple answer is the code that will unlock almost everything you need to know about selling to executives.

First, this executive tells us that he expects salespeople to offer suggestions for his business instead of hearing the all-too-common "show up and throw up" sales pitch or a glad-hand social call. In today's wireless world, executives know more about your offering and your competitor's products than you can tell them in 60 minutes. They don't need a walking brochure, and if they want a friend, they can buy a dog. Instead, the CIO tells us to be professional, be conversant with the executive's business problems (or opportunities), and prepare a call plan that delivers some level of value to him.

As Gordon Gekko tells enthusiastic pitcher Bud Fox in Oliver Stone's film *Wall Street*: "You had what it took to get into my office, Sport; the question is, do you have what it takes to stay?"

Second, this CIO is saying that we'd better be prepared to tell him things he can't get from his own people, and that he wants to know how his business compares in the market. Is his company leading the curve, or is it falling behind? What do best practices look like? We need to know enough about how the executive's company does things today to be able to offer opinions about how it can do better. "You stop sending me information, and you start getting me some," was Gordon Gekko's next challenge to Bud Fox. "Surprise me." And so it is for us.

This CIO concludes with the ray of hope that a salesperson who is doing these things has a shot at standing out in the crowd. Note that he doesn't say that he wants a *vendor* relationship. His purchasing department can own those. What the executive is looking for is a *Trusted Advisor* relationship with salespeople who can speak on the executive's terms, discuss the same metrics, and add value to the thought process.

Are you up to the challenge? Our invitation to you is to read on, find out where you rank, and learn how to climb the totem pole.

As you achieve greater professional success using these guides, we trust you will share your own war stories with us to include in future reprints of this book! Send them to us at Stories@CXO-Selling.com.

Now, start your engines . . .

Acknowledgments

Every business book is a distillation of experiences and associations, and this one is no exception. We therefore thank our students, staff, and professional colleagues who have contributed in so many ways to the insights that make up this publication.

We acknowledge the collegial support of Jay E. Klompmaker, Ph.D., of the University of North Carolina; Alston Gardner, the visionary who founded Target Marketing Systems; and supporters from Hewlett-Packard who helped direct the 1995 Selling to Senior Executives initial study upon which some of our findings are based.

Encouragement from the international community is always appreciated. Of particular note has been support from Kevin Wilson of the Sales Research Trust Ltd UK; Lisa Napolitano, who headed the Strategic Account Management Association (SAMA) so well for so long; Steve Andersen of Performance Methods Inc.; Anne An, former director of the Hewlett-Packard Business School in Beijing, China; and author Jerry Stapleton, whose ideas about becoming a true business resource are right on the money.

ACKNOWLEDGMENTS

Of the many hundreds of sales professionals who have shared stories and anecdotes about selling to executives, we single out the unique personalities of Millard Allen, Charles Bates, Alan Beck, Doug Boyle, Chuck Cagno, Jan Feddersen, Howard Freeman, John Harris, Helen Harwood, Karen Jackson, Bobby Knight, Doug Knispel, Ian Laidlaw, Matt Lovegrove, Lisa Nirell, Jeff Pace, Bruce Parkhurst, Erwin Peter, Stu Price, Jess Ray, Dennis Roberson, Mar Robinson, Spring Weng, Ronnie Wimberley, and our dear late friend Clare Sutton. A special thank you to Dom DiMauro for his many ideas and lifelong friendship.

The guidance and strong editorial contributions from our publisher transformed the manuscript into a comprehensive whole. We appreciate the insight, the talents, and the tremendous amount of work given to this book. We also must thank John Outler for handling the graphics and software that have always been associated with this project.

Finally, our everlasting thanks to our spouses and children for putting up with our long hours and time on the road and in the air.

Chapter 1

When Do Executives Get Involved in the Decision Process?

Selling to senior-level executives requires a different set of skills and strategies from the more traditional departmental-level transactional sale. Until the early 1980s, product was king. When a company introduced a new product, it was in many cases proprietary, allowing the company to get a lot of mileage out of being the "best in class" or "leading edge" before a competitor got around to leapfrogging it with an alternative offering.

Because of strong product differentiation, manufacturers dominated the business environment. For them, the standard go-to-market approach was a direct sales force, whose key functions were to provide basic product information, a point of contact with the vendor, and a human face to associate with the product. This sales force typically was made up of geographically assigned salespeople, each of whom called on a large number of accounts within a particular territory. This sales force most often sold to operations-level employees within individual departments like procurement or purchasing.

In the mid-1980s, priorities shifted. Customers were knowledgeable about and comfortable with existing products, and they no longer needed a direct sales force to supply product information. Now they wanted low prices. Not altogether by coincidence, India and China stepped in as offshore providers of lower-cost manufacturing and services, and western producers flocked to them in a bid to meet their customers' demands for savings while preserving their own margin. Supply Chain Management, Business Process Reengineering, Total Quality Management, and Six Sigma had their roots in this wave of stripping cost and inefficiency from the buy-build-sell chain. The shift to lower-cost channels of distribution—or multichannel marketing— also began in this era, spawning hundreds of thousands of call centers, resellers, and online ordering portals in many industries.

At the same time, customers began to wonder how they could extract even more value from their suppliers, and they woke up to the fact that salespeople who were desperate to make a sale could be given the task of providing free consulting on ways to solve the more complex business problems. All of us who sold in that era needed knowledge of our own products, how they fitted into our customer's operation, and how to assemble other components of a solution using products and services from third-party suppliers—we had now become solution architects and partner relationship managers, for whom selling a solution became a matter of juggling multiple relationships across our own company, the customer's company, and other vendors' companies. We were moving from the neat model of being a representative of one brand to being a broker for many products, services, and stakeholder agendas. To paraphrase from the tale of globalization that Thomas Friedman paints in *The Lexus and the Olive Tree* (HarperCollins, 1999):

> Sony moved from the stereo and CD market into the digital camera market where a 3.5-inch diskette became the film, the computer printer became the photo-processing store, and email became the post office. Sony learned it could be Sony, Kodak and Federal Express all at the same time as a one-stop business solution. Kodak responded to the challenge by promoting itself as a personal computer company. Compaq and Dell responded by saying computers were now commodities and they'd evolved to selling "business solutions." Accounting-consulting firms that had previously held business solutions as their bread and butter were less worried about the computer companies and more concerned by the likes of Goldman Sachs and other investment bankers that started selling tax and investment advice. You could read about these trends in books available at Borders stores, which now sold CDs—Sony's original market. Everyone is now in everyone else's business.

That's the world of "business solutions," and by definition it demanded that as salespeople, we had to move beyond the operations and middle managers if we were to be heard above all the noise—we had to be more visible at the executive level.

Then in the 1990s another trend emerged. Business solutions that had once seemed complicated to put together, and hence needed the input of salespeople, now became commonplace. Customers got the hang of it, identified the best vendors, and started compiling these solutions themselves. The internal departments responsible for building these multivendor solutions started to get very good at it. Some of them were spun off as separate businesses; one-stop-shop systems process integration was born in the information technology market, and integration then spread in different forms to other industries.

Salespeople had educated the market on how to do it, and they were now competing with their very own customers for services work that had become more profitable than selling the product itself. With the rise of Amazon.com, eBay, and other portals, the commoditization of high-value services only accelerated. We remember not so many years ago people saying: "Okay, so we get that customers can buy PCs over the Internet now. But they'll never buy something as complicated as servers without seeing a rep!" Then came Dell.com.

BUILDING A FOUNDATION OF C-SUITE KNOWLEDGE

Recognizing this trend in 1995 and looking for answers, an Atlanta-based sales training company called Target Marketing Systems (creator of the Target Account Selling workshop) conducted a study in conjunction with Hewlett-Packard and the University of North Carolina's Kenan-Flagler Business School in Chapel Hill. This research was managed by Steve Bistritz, Ed.D. (a coauthor of this book), who sought to discover what salespeople had to do in the Internet age to remain relevant to senior executives, and what factors most influenced the executive decision-making process.

The original purpose of the research project was to examine not only how professional, business-to-business salespeople interacted and interfaced with CXO-level executives in client organizations, but how they built lasting, trust-based relationships with those same client executives. In addition, there was an interest in learning from the executive's perspective what salespeople had to do to conduct and deliver effective meetings with executives. The initial study had an interesting origin: coincidentally, Hewlett-Packard was at the same time attempting to establish a new national sales organization that would focus on selling to senior client executives, and the company genuinely wanted to understand what it took for those salespeople to gain the trust and credibility of those executives.

From its perspective, HP was actually trying to determine how its salespeople could ultimately come to be perceived as trusted advisors to those same client executives. The company decided to cosponsor the study and did so by contributing to the cost of the study process and participating in the planning and execution of the study itself. By the way, today the phrase *trusted advisor* has become an overused expression in the selling environment, but back in 1995 it was not commonly used, and HP's use of the phrase may have been one of the early examples of its use.

The rationale for Target Marketing Systems to cosponsor the study was that the company was in the midst of developing an instructor-led workshop for professional salespeople on selling to executives and was interested in determining the best ways for salespeople to create, maintain, and leverage relationships with senior-level executives in client organizations. In perusing sales journals and the existing literature in 1995, the original research manager could not find any articles written by CXO-level executives that discussed their relationships with professional salespeople or why they would want to meet with those salespeople. At that time, most books and articles on the topic of selling to executives were written by salespeople or sales executives and focused on the *salesperson's* anecdotal experience in dealing with senior client executives, and a literature search did not find any books or articles published in that time frame that spoke about creating and establishing those relationships from the *executive's* perspective. Many of these books contained numerous war stories from the author's vast experience, but none of them were written from the perspective of the client executive.

Interest also developed at the University of North Carolina's Business School because a professor of marketing at the school, Dr. Jay Klompmaker, was also a member of the advisory board for Target Marketing Systems. He saw the research project as an outstanding opportunity for four of his graduate students in the MBA program—all of whom had previous experience as business-to-business salespeople—to participate in a practical and useful study that could make a significant contribution to the sales profession. Their participation in the study process subsequently became part of the practicum requirements for the MBA. He also duplicated the literature search on the topic and reached the identical conclusions about the lack of available information about selling to executives that was written from the executive's perspective.

Preparation for the project interviews took nearly six months; a detailed questionnaire was developed for the interviews, a list of potential client executives to be interviewed was created, and practice interviews were planned and conducted. Numerous iterations of the survey questionnaire, combined with a series of practice interviews, resulted in a concise but effective survey. The executives to be interviewed came mainly from established executive-level contacts of employees within Target Marketing Systems and Hewlett-Packard. The executives themselves were not prescreened in any manner, except that each executive had to be willing to commit to an hour of his time for the actual survey process. The criteria for selecting the specific executives were that they clearly had to be senior-level line executives, typically at the vice president or CXO level. It is important to note that purchasing and procurement executives were specifically excluded from the survey.

The experienced sales professionals on the MBA track at UNC interviewed more than 60 senior executives, ranging from vice presidents to chairmen. These interviews were conducted in person or by telephone and lasted up to 60 minutes. The reason for conducting interviews in this manner was that we wanted to make certain that the responses were coming directly from the executives themselves. If we had sent an executive our questionnaire on this topic, it could easily have ultimately been completed by the executive's administrative assistant or secretary or by a lower-level executive. In our opinion, this would have compromised the process. In addition, we wanted to be able to capture some of the anecdotal comments made by the executive, and this could be done only in face-to-face or telephone interviews.

Executives were selected from diverse industries, including transportation, textiles, telecommunications, utilities, financial services, technology, printing, and office furniture. Four years later, in the spring of 1999, the same study was expanded in collaboration with the Center for Business and Industrial Marketing at Georgia State University in Atlanta, with more than 125 senior executives being surveyed in total.

In preparing for the initial interviews with executives, Hewlett-Packard arranged for each of the four MBA students to conduct a series of practice interviews with some of HP's own senior executives. These in-person practice interviews took place at HP's corporate headquarters in California. The purpose of these practice interviews was to carefully vet the questionnaire that had been developed, make certain that there were no questions that could be misinterpreted or issues that could arise, and also confirm that the MBA students were thoroughly prepared to conduct effective 60-minute interviews with client executives.

To ensure that the process was conducted appropriately, the research manager accompanied the MBA students to each of the practice interviews to validate the process and help set the tone for each interview. We also wanted to verify that each of the four MBA students was prepared, confident, and competent, because their next step was a live interview with a senior-level client executive. These initial interviews were very successful and provided us with additional insight into how to conduct the interviews with client executives, as well as how to treat the executives during the process. The executives at HP who participated in the practice interviews also told us that the process provided value to them because they gained additional insight into how they could perhaps work more effectively with the salespeople they dealt with on an ongoing basis.

To test for cultural variance, the research was expanded in 2005 by Nic Read (this book's other coauthor), who at the time was president of the sales consulting firm SalesLabs and an advisor to the Hewlett-Packard Business School in Beijing, China. Hewlett-Packard again proved invaluable in the research process. Its business school in China, in concert with Ivy League universities, provided executive MBA programs to Chinese executives. Over a two-year period, when executives and senior managers finished a course of study, they were asked to complete a detailed questionnaire about how they viewed China's entry into the World Trade Organization in terms of the challenges it created for local companies that needed to raise their standards to become globally competitive, the implications for them as leaders, and what they looked for from the salespeople and vendors who were knocking on China's door with new solutions. Nic's team collected surveys and interviewed more than 400 chairmen, vice presidents, and managing directors of Chinese state-owned enterprises and multinational companies in the insurance, biotech, pharmaceutical, telecommunications, banking, airline, steel, and information technology industries. This study lifted the total sample of executives who were interviewed to more than 500, from which surprisingly consistent findings were extrapolated on how executives get involved in the buying cycle and what salespeople need to do to gain their trust and create value.

The following sections reveal what we learned.

EXECUTIVE INVOLVEMENT IN THE BUYING CYCLE

Salespeople who want to build relationships with executives must enter the picture early in the buying cycle because this is when 80 percent of executives usually or always become involved in significant purchase decisions (see Figure 1.1).

The executives' motivation at this stage is to understand current business issues, establish project objectives, and set the overall project strategy to deal with what might be termed a *breakthrough initiative*: something that is critical to the client's success because of significant payback from its implementation or serious consequences if action is delayed or not taken.

According to one executive from the office furniture industry:

I get involved in the "what" and "why," not so much the "how." At the beginning, I put in a lot of personal time making sure the project's on the right track and moving in the right direction.

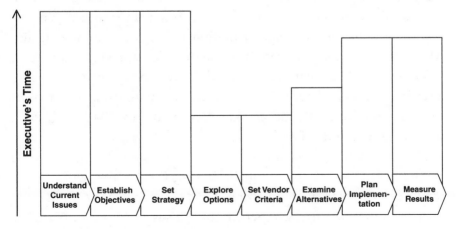

Figure 1.1 Executive Involvement in the Buying Cycle

Another executive from the airline industry told us:

I'm planning now for how my business will look ten years from now. It's difficult to forecast on our own, so we depend on the ideas of suppliers and partners in the same industry, on the belief that separately we might be wrong, but together we're probably right. Vendors who can't engage in that forward thinking don't get off the ground with me.

Comments regarding executive involvement in the early phase of the buying cycle were consistent in each of our three studies.

During the middle phase of the buying cycle, executives tend to reduce their involvement and delegate decisions to subordinates or committees. Executives in the survey said that once a clear vision is set, it's time to empower the people below them. "Once we've defined the parameters, my tendency is to get out of the way," said one respondent. Most of the executives never or only occasionally involve themselves at this stage.

However, all three research studies confirmed that executives get significantly involved once again late in the buying cycle to evaluate whether the vendors can really deliver the original vision and to measure the results of the implementation. They want to understand whether the vendor delivered the value that was originally committed. They also told us that the closer they get to the contract being awarded, the less they are likely to supersede the recommendations of the evaluation team; the purchasing decision has usually already been made in their minds, if not on paper.

Do you see the problem here?

The middle to late phase of the buying cycle is the period when senior executives in medium-size to large companies are *least likely* to open their calendar to a salesperson. But this is when most invitations to quote and submit proposals happen. Salespeople who get their first scent of a deal at this stage and expect to "meet the boss" are usually frustrated by the difficulty of doing so. If you are able to gain access to the right executive early enough in the buying process, your efforts are likely to be rewarded. But don't expect marketing to line up those meetings for you. Here's why.

Executives are increasingly using the Internet to inform their views, but they do not type in the category of solution because this early in the process, they're not educated enough to know where a solution will come from. Instead, they search based on the problem confronting them. This is a challenge for marketers if their search engine optimization program uses only tag-words that describe their solution (which is most of them).

Try this experiment. Imagine that you are an executive and you're early in your buying cycle. You don't know what the solution will be yet, but you know that your problems are "customer growth" and "declining revenue." You want to see who can solve those problems.

Type these two phrases into a search engine and write down the top three hits for each. Here's what we found doing this experiment on Google:

"customer growth": 301,000 hits

1. A direct mail and advertising agency
2. A research company in the retail consumer goods space
3. A software company offering real-time Web site reporting

"declining revenue": 76,900 hits

1. A 2007 *Wall Street Journal* article on advertising
2. A 2008 *Reuters* article about a printing press company
3. A 2008 news article about a diet company

The top three hits for each problem are random. This is why many salespeople don't get invited to talk to executives early—the executives are looking for ideas about solving their problems, but most companies' search engine listings are focused on how the seller sees the world, not how the latent buyer sees it.

Now do the same experiment again, but this time think like a marketing person who can't see beyond her product category (which, as we'll discuss in the next chapter, is most of them). We randomly chose the categories "customer relationship management" and "account management" as solutions to the previously cited problems of "customer growth" and "declining revenue":

"customer relationship management": 14,500,000 hits

1. A customer relationship management (CRM) software company
2. A CRM software company
3. A CRM software company

"account management": 8,520,000 hits

1. A sales training company
2. A sales training company
3. A sales training company

Look at the comparison. We get 377,000 hits when our executive is first exploring these problems and is most open to new ideas (early in the buying cycle). But as we've seen, most of these hits were random and failed to connect to relevant sellers. It's only after the buyer is already educated about a product category (usually the middle of the buying process, when executives are least likely to be involved) that most Internet marketing connects buyers to the right sellers, in this case 23 million of them who were marketing their wares using industry-speak, not prospect-speak. Ever wondered why RFPs are so competitive? Or why so many evaluators have already pigeon-holed you before your first meeting? Or why so few executive prospects spend their time camping on your doorstep? Now you know.

We recently attended an enormous marketing event staged by an industry leader. A record number of prospects, customers, partners, and media representatives attended, a bevy of athletic girls in baseball caps gave directions to more than 1,000 visitors, and the coffee was hot and free-flowing. The company had spent real money on this event, and it showed. Anticipation built as huge screens counted down to the opening address, punctuated by spinning lights and rock music. When the vice president of marketing mounted the stage, he delivered a truly passionate and charismatic presentation about how his company was redefining its industry, and about how its customers were no longer satisfied with being sold a bunch of products and widgets; they wanted solutions to their business problems. Our curiosity was piqued by the expectation that we were about to see a company really get this right.

The vice president then revealed the next slide, which showed the company's products grouped into neat boxes, and declared that the company was going to market with several modular solutions, labeled in industry-speak. We didn't hear the rest of his speech. Instead we sat pondering why it is that so many clever companies come so close to getting it right, and then choke at the finish line. This company was clearly on the right path, but it was no more than one step away from its product despite dressing it up with the word *solution* 26 times before we zoned out. To truly focus on solutions means to solve problems. To talk about problems is to abandon the self-indulgence of promoting your products. It's not a comfortable place for most marketers to be. Which is why next year, when this company runs the same event, it will probably be attended by the same gearheads who were attracted by all the industry-speak, and it will never be discovered by executives who are searching in prospect-speak.

All three research studies told us that 80 percent of executives get involved early in their buyer's journey to prioritize projects and set the vision. We know they use the Internet to explore options for solving their problem. And we've seen that most companies fail to position

Executive's View of	Stage 1	Stage 2	Stage 3	Stage 4
Your Objective	Make a Sale	Make a Contribution	Provide Insight	Provide Leverage
Your Contribution to the Company	Disruption to the Executive's Business Day	Logical Thinker	Critical Thinker	Strategic Resource
Your Relationship with the Executive	Intermittent	Interactive	Interesting	Interdependent
Your Status	Commodity Supplier	Emerging Resource	Problem Solver	Trusted Advisor
Access to the Executive	Sent Down	Considered	Occasional	Continual

Figure 1.2 Four Stages of Sales Proficiency

themselves around problems, and so don't get on the executive's radar early enough.

This means that unless your marketing machine changes its approach to lead generation, which we discuss in the next chapter, you need to rely on good old-fashioned prospecting and selling skills to reach executives early in their buying cycle. To pull that off, you need sales proficiency that's beyond the capabilities of most salespeople.

But you can learn this.

There are four stages of sales proficiency that you may pass through during your sales career, which we'll cover in the next section (see Figure 1.2).

FOUR STAGES OF SALES PROFICIENCY
1. Commodity Supplier

Salespeople who are Commodity Suppliers see the world through a pair of product glasses. They believe that if they can just get the opportunity to show their product or service, the features of their product or their brand will help them succeed. Their world extends little further than the execution of tactics such as setting up meetings, making sales presentations, giving demonstrations, and writing proposals. As a result, they rarely get involved early enough in a sale to create opportunities with an executive buyer.

We recently participated in a conference call between one such salesperson who was attempting to make a sale and a Symantec vice president in California. The sales rep boasted before the call: "I don't need to know their business, their issues, or anything about them. We've got the best product on the market, and that speaks for itself." To his credit, when we suggested that he might prepare for the call by at least checking the firm's Web site for the latest news, he spent a few minutes browsing. However, to our chagrin, his first words were: "So what's this new initiative I see listed all over your Web site? It looks like this SYMC project is pretty important!" SYMC is Symantec's stock market symbol!

This rep's belief that product was king was so deeply entrenched that he never felt the need to understand the client's world and believed that clients existed only to help him meet his quota. Those operations-level customers who agreed to see him considered this rep nothing more than the guy to call when they needed a discount on an order that they'd already decided to place. They also knew that he'd always buy the drinks when they had people in town, so they would regularly dent his expense account under the guise of *account management*. Consequently, he was one of the highest-selling yet least profitable salespeople in his company.

The executives we interviewed typically called this type of salesperson a "product expert," and one that they would rarely waste their time on. One said: "If all someone can do is talk features, functions, and benefits, then he's going to turn me off pretty fast." Another complained: "At the end of these meetings, I feel like I was interrupted, that they wasted my time."

Many executives indicated that they would immediately refer these salespeople to either executives or staff members at lower levels of the organization who can deal with the product and technical issues that they perceive to be the only issues that these Commodity Suppliers are comfortable discussing.

While, through diligence and consistent efforts, the salesperson who has a Commodity Supplier relationship may have been able to schedule an initial meeting with an executive, her inability to discuss the issues that are critical to executives converts an extraordinary opportunity into wasted time for both the executive and the salesperson. At that point, the salesperson's ability to gain further access to the same senior-level executive becomes questionable, at best.

Salespeople typically only get one shot at impressing an executive, and Commodity Suppliers seldom score a second appointment. However, tactics that the salesperson can implement at this point are worth mentioning. To demonstrate some level of follow-through that might impress the executive, a salesperson should do two things to try to secure another meeting with him, namely, (1) ask the executive for an introduction to the appropriate lower-level person, and (2) ask the executive for a follow-on meeting to review the results.

Asking the executive for an introduction to the lower-level executive or staff person shows the person at the lower level the importance of the meeting, and asking the senior-level executive for a follow-up meeting may represent one way for the salesperson to secure return access.

However, don't feel we're saying that this type of selling is wrong. Commodity Suppliers have their place under the right circumstances. As former General Electric CEO Jack Welch said: "You can't grow long-term if you can't eat short-term."[1] Selling like a Commodity Supplier on deals where the customer has a fast buying cycle is exactly the right thing to do. These deals don't need to be overengineered; they need to be closed before the competition finds them. A dozen small deals now is better than any large deal in the future.

Selling like a Commodity Supplier is also the right approach when the name of the game is meeting demand in what might be described as a hypergrowth market. This occurs under two different conditions.

The first condition is when a new market opens up in a developing nation like China, where consumers with new money are buying well-known brand products, and distributors supplying this burgeoning middle class are looking for reliable suppliers who can ship product as quickly as it runs off the shelves. But beware: while market demand combined with stable supply and keen pricing usually guarantees a long and successful run—clever marketing, pricing wars, or new features can easily shift loyalty to alternative brands just as quickly because a commodity market is driven largely by fickle consumer behavior.

The second condition is when a product moves from being the technical darling of early adopters to achieving widespread popularity. This is what author-consultant Geoffrey Moore called the Tornado,[2] based in part on the pioneering work of the late Everett M. Rogers[3] on how innovation spreads to mass acceptance. In this stage of hyper-growth, companies need to keep up with demand by selling quickly and moving on to the next sale—again the domain of the Commodity Supplier.

But in developed markets with risk-averse buyers, a lack of higher-level skills makes Commodity Suppliers flare up on the radar of senior executives, who routinely avoid them as a waste of time, usually sending them down to deal with people at a lower level.

2. Emerging Resource

A salesperson who is an Emerging Resource might get involved in a company's decision process after being tested as a Commodity Supplier for some time, typically at an operations or middle management level. These people have earned their spurs at the lower level and won the right to do more work as a result of their track record.

Becoming an Emerging Resource is a negotiation process in which Commodity Suppliers sell their value beyond pure product to other services and resources that they bring to the relationship. Once they are convinced of this value, customers grant the Emerging Resource the type of contract that keeps competitors out of an account and widens the "license to hunt" for a specified time in return for preferential pricing or service. This is the same principle seen in politics when nations ratify their relationship by signing trade agreements that confer "preferred trading partner" status on one or both parties. It's based on the perception that transacting with Emerging Resources is less risky and lower cost than receiving submissions from countless unknown suppliers each time a need arises.

Emerging Resources stand out from Commodity Suppliers when they do their homework to identify what advantages can be created for the customer by awarding preference to a single supplier. This has to be more than a generic value proposition. It's based on knowing how the customer orders and who else the customer trades with, and being able to spot the inefficiencies that having a single one-stop vendor can solve. It's also about having the patience to build credentials in small ways to earn the right to pitch this proposition and get credit as a logical thinker.

When the National Football League (NFL) announced its new prime-time broadcast deals in April 2005, *Monday Night Football* was taken away from ABC and handed back to NBC, which had lost the account eight years earlier.[4] The deal extended to NBC's parent company, General Electric. Along with securing broadcast rights for NFL games, General Electric became an Emerging Resource to the NFL and all of its teams for health care, financial services, lighting, and security equipment. It emerged as a resource that added value on multiple fronts.

3. Problem Solver

It's at the Problem Solver level of sales proficiency that salespeople shift from an internal focus on their products to an external focus on the customer's wider world. As a result, they start to see and talk about issues that aren't immediately connected to a current deal, but rather have yet to be handled. Problem Solver salespeople begin to understand their customers' business problems and seek an approach that will solve those problems; they shift their sights away from their own product long enough to listen to the customer and understand the larger environment within which the product must operate. Their ideas are usually forward-looking and more strategic, which qualifies them to meet with executives who are looking to the same horizon for answers.

Executives meeting with Problem Solver salespeople usually have a better opinion of them than they do of Commodity Supplier and Emerging Resource salespeople. One executive told us that a Problem Solver salesperson is: "Someone who is a potential resource. During the presentation, we explored several creative ideas together. I'll take these ideas under consideration and possibly meet with him again."

4. Trusted Advisor

After a few years of experience honing their craft, some salespeople level out at the Problem Solver level. So what can they do to stand out from the pack of other Problem Solvers? Trusted Advisors focus on the value of a personal relationship with the executive. They develop this relationship by understanding the executive as a person first, then recognizing the executive's broad vision for her business. They advise on the common obstacles to avoid, suggest proven best practices, and build relationships within the political dynamic of the executive's inner circle, that is, those trusted lieutenants inside and outside of the company that the executive turns to for advice. They serve as a compass and a mine detector by providing insight and foresight that the executive isn't already tapped into.

The executives cited the continuing value of dealing with salespeople who had obviously helped to solve similar business problems for other customers. One executive said: "Some of these salespeople can relate to business problems at a very high level. They understand that their solution may not be a panacea, but they deliver business value by helping me explore various options. My objective is to discuss my business problems with them and develop realistic solutions, not to see a slick sales presentation."

Another executive cited the salesperson's ability to draw on internal or even external partner resources as a way of possibly solving the problem as a key indicator of business value. She said, "The salesperson I meet with should provide me with the benefit of his experience, but also be able to secure the additional resources required to provide a broader view of the solution."

Salespeople who operate at the Trusted Advisor level of a business relationship with multiple executives in several organizations quickly develop skills that can be transferred from customer to customer. Senior-level executives in those organizations immediately recognize the salespeople who regularly connect with executives at their level because they can sense the business knowledge, confidence, and competence that those salespeople demonstrate. It's as if the executives have a sixth sense, and can spot the salespeople who are continually dealing with their peers in other organizations.

Of all of the traits demonstrated, being prepared for the meeting with the executive is one that is both highly valued and quickly recognized. There is no substitute for having a substantial understanding of the customer's industry, her company, and the customer executive herself. Developing this insight into the customer is also one of the easiest ways to develop a genuine and lasting rapport with senior-level executives. It can also shorten the salesperson's sales cycle because it quickly differentiates you from your competitors. This knowledge enables you to be in a better position to serve as a consultant to the customer, contributing your insights and creating the foundation for a long-term, collaborative relationship. And most importantly, this demonstration of business knowledge enables the salesperson to convert a meeting with an executive into an extraordinary opportunity, as well as continued access to the executive.

One executive described a Trusted Advisor salesperson as: "Someone I consider a business consultant who gave me ideas about my business that even my own people didn't come up with. As a result, I felt we had a business meeting where she demonstrated some compelling business value and also gave me some reasons why I should grant her continued access to me."

This continued access to senior executives is critical to building the long-term relationships required to consistently succeed. Trusted Advisor salespeople don't wait to jump in at the middle of the buying cycle, which is when Commodity Supplier salespeople first get alerted to a deal—they get involved earlier to help the client identify and assess options, then determine the most effective way to address his high-priority issues.

Earlier we cited an example of how NBC and General Electric became an Emerging Resource for the NFL. There is another famous deal that was pulled off by NBC that illustrates what it takes to be a Trusted Advisor.

The broadcast rights to the Olympic Games are usually awarded in four-year packages, one Olympics at a time. NBC, ABC, Fox, and other broadcasters routinely compete in that four-year cycle to win the coveted contract. But NBC's Dick Ebersol blew that model out of the water by locking up the broadcast rights for both Sydney in 2000 and Salt Lake City in 2002, followed quickly by a second deal for all Olympic coverage through to Beijing in 2008. It was an unprecedented deal in broadcasting history. *Sports Illustrated* magazine featured an excellent article on Ebersol's deal in its Christmas Day edition in 1995.[5] Here are a few outtakes that explain key principles by which Trusted Advisors like Ebersol operate:

- Trusted Advisors determine what the object of their affection wants to hear. They know what these people want to hear because they are consistently better prepared and better informed than their rivals. "Ebersol rises at 6:15 every morning and reads four daily newspapers."

- Trusted Advisors know the personal agendas of their customers and find ways to *leverage their company's resources* to deliver what their customers want. "Ebersol came up with an offer to broadcast a weekly Olympic magazine show from 1996 to 2002. He knew coverage in non-Olympic years held appeal for Juan Antonio Samaranch" (then the president of the International Olympic Committee).

- Trusted Advisors listen for little clues. "Samaranch congratulated Ebersol on the 'stability' they had achieved and on the 'partnership' they had forged. Ebersol was struck by Samaranch's repeated references to the long-term nature of their relationship," and sensed that his customer might be interested in a much longer-term contract than the two Olympics already signed up.

- Trusted Advisors create deals that offer personal value as well as sound commercial value, and they do so in a way that makes the buyer and the seller *interdependent*. Ebersol came up with what was nicknamed the Sunset Project—a deal for not two but five Olympic Games that created long-term financial stability for the IOC and a legacy for Samaranch to leave behind.

As one Trusted Advisor salesperson explained: "Instead of just reacting to a customer's request for a quote, I start becoming more inquisitive about why the customer may want something and the eventual effects of buying my product or service."

Being "inquisitive" the way this Trusted Advisor suggests means understanding the executive's current issues and helping him establish objectives for his broad business interests before setting a strategy to explore external capabilities from you. To make that happen, you need to do your homework on the customer, his business, and his industry.

Where do you rank? What do you need to do differently to advance? It's food for thought.

Chapter Summary

Let's summarize what we've discussed in this chapter about the first question in our research: "When do executives get involved in the buying process?" Let's break it down to the top three messages:

1. *Get in early.*

   Executives get involved in purchasing decisions early, when the original vision is being set and before the task of finding suppliers is delegated. They use the Internet to inform their thought process about the problem they face. Most marketing fails to help them find you at this stage, so you need to rely on your selling skills. However, if your marketing department sends out problem-focused messages that attract the executives who face those problems, and sends a series of repetitive wake-up calls to help them recognize that (a) they have a problem and (b) you can solve that problem, then your ability to plug into the start of the executive decision process will improve.

2. *Focus on their breakthrough initiative.*

   Use your knowledge of the executive's business drivers to identify her *breakthrough initiative*—the single most important problem or opportunity she needs to invest in where your products or services can make a demonstrable difference. Breakthrough initiatives are typically identified only at the executive level, meaning that people at lower levels of the organization may not even be aware of them until they are formalized as a project. By the time they become formal and other suppliers are invited to bid, the executive's views of both solution and vendor have often already been set if one supplier has demonstrated thought leadership from the start.

3. *Meet with executives to measure the results of the implementation.*

Our research told us that senior-level executives want to meet with salespeople and review the value that the salespeople's solutions have delivered to their organization—so take advantage of that opportunity. Don't assume that executives always have a clear understanding of the value you delivered—make certain you communicate that value directly to them in a succinct manner.

In addition, consider conducting annual meetings with senior-level executives to review the value you deliver to them on a recurring basis. This could elevate their view of you to either Problem Solver or Trusted Advisor status.

A Brave New World for Sales and Marketing

In the previous chapter, we established that as salespeople strive to retain profitable customers and win new ones, they often need to gain access to and establish credibility with senior executives. These stakeholders are often among the first to see an opportunity to improve their operation through the purchase of external goods and services, and they nurture such ideas from concept to budget. In small and medium-sized companies, this same person may stay on as project leader or serve on the evaluation committee. But in large enterprises, the executive may see his job as complete when he's handed over the task of selecting a supplier to the purchasing officers. After that happens, the ability of a salesperson to connect with the executive who initiated a project is restricted by the project managers to whom the task is delegated.

Good salespeople know that if their first entry into a deal is through a formal request for proposal (RFP) or tender, they've already lost the upper hand. They attempt to counter the tender process by offering the quid pro quo of providing the requested documentation in return for interviews with key people, accompanied by the suggestion that by doing so, they'll be better able to prepare a solution that meets all the buyer's needs. This sounds good on the surface, but purchasing managers that we've talked to tell us that under the terms of a tender process (especially when selling to government agencies), if they grant this dispensation to one vendor, they must do so for all or risk the appearance of playing favorites—a matter of corporate governance. Purchasers also point out that when salespeople ask to meet other stakeholders, what they really hear is: "I want to interview people to determine your needs because you probably didn't scope this for me to win" or "I want to build a base of supporters because I don't believe you will buy my price except under political duress." How perceptive of them.

It is therefore not surprising to hear buyers make the legitimate request that we route all communication through them and not call over their heads. We should also not be surprised that by the time we get invited to the party, much of the buying process has already been completed, with buyers using the Internet to window-shop, create a short list, and make comparisons.

The Internet heralded what *New York Times* columnist Thomas Friedman calls "the democratization of information." In his book *The Lexus and the Olive Tree* (HarperCollins, 1999), Friedman cites *USA Today*'s technology columnist Kevin Maney as saying:

> As a world-changing invention, the Net echoes many of the characteristics of the printing press. It brings a dramatic drop in the cost of creating, sending and storing information while vastly increasing its availability. It breaks information monopolies.

It's these "information monopolies" that salespeople have depended on for leverage in the buyer-seller relationship for 200 years. Within a decade, the Internet has become a counterstroke to the customer's dependence on salespeople for information, especially at the executive level.

How did this happen?

In the late 1990s, marketing started getting the hang of HTML and packed Web sites full of information about the company's credentials, product information, customer testimonials, and even its rate cards. Marketing didn't realize it at the time, but these Web sites were stripping away what had formerly been a large part of a salesperson's role as a knowledge provider. Because of the *infoglut* on most corporate Web sites, many customers no longer need the diagnosis of a salesperson—they can self-medicate.

But only if they know that they need to find you.

The problem many sales pros encounter is that the majority of prospects aren't actively searching. They have latent or chronic problems, but they've learned to live with them, and they need to be awakened to the fact that they need to change before they can be pointed in the right direction. And that's not something that marketing departments are generally good at doing anymore. But it wasn't always this way.

Modern marketing began with the printing press in the seventeenth century. The first newspapers sold space for print advertising, which was extended to direct mail and mail-order catalogs in the 1850s. In the 1920s, radio was invented, and companies sponsored shows in return for their products being mentioned. This same format was used when television shows went on the air in the 1940s. With few exceptions, the products being pitched through print and electronic media were all household consumer goods like soap powder, toothpaste, deodorant, apparel, kitchenware, food and beverages, travel, and automobiles.

Today's consumer goods exist in well-defined product categories. Customers know what the product is and what it does, and the decision to buy is based on personal preferences concerning its style, taste, price, prestige, utility, or novelty. Marketing of these products focuses less on "why do I need it?" and more on "which one should I buy?" because consumers are already educated about the product category and its application in their life. Choosing between Product A and Product B is therefore the impulse that marketing targets.

But in the century between 1850 and 1950, industrialization was inventing products that had never existed before. These goods were not in categories that consumers were familiar with, and their value wasn't as self-evident as that of products today. For example, today's consumer doesn't think twice about having a refrigerator; people consider it to be a standard feature of a modern kitchen.

Yet in 1932, Electrolux had to run advertisements to convince people that they needed to stop storing perishable food in an ice cellar and put a gas-powered refrigerator inside their kitchen instead.

The Electrolux advertisement in Figure 2.1 shows a woman wearing horse blinders, with the headline "Blinders . . . because she shies at new ideas." The text opens with: "Flying machines, horseless

Blinders... *because she* *Shies* At New Ideas

FLYING MACHINES, horseless carriages they had their skeptics. Every new idea, every great advance, does. Electrolux is no exception.

We don't mind that. For though Electrolux is four years old, has enjoyed a phenomenal success and is today in hundreds of thousands of homes, it is still the new idea, the big radical improvement in automatic refrigerators.

All we ask is that your go and see Electrolux with your eyes wide open. Judge the facts at first hand.

You will find that Electrolux not only freezes ice cubes quickly and provides perfect constant cold always, but does this without sound, without machinery, and at much less cost than any other refrigerator.

Is it any wonder that Electrolux sales in 1931 were far ahead of 1930?

You certainly owe it to yourself to see this remarkable refrigerator that has so greatly changed the old order of things. It is on display at the showroom of your gas company.

And if you'd like complete information by mail, write to us direct for free literature. Electrolux Refrigerator Sales, Inc., Evansville, Indiana.

ELECTROLUX
THE *Gas* REFRIGERATOR

The old order changeth — a tiny gas flame takes the place of all moving parts

Figure 2.1 "New" Product Marketing Using Shame as a Motivator

Source: Good Housekeeping, 1932.

carriages—they had their skeptics. . . . All we ask is that you go and see Electrolux with your eyes wide open."

The image and headline imply the following messages:

- "If you don't move with the times, you are old-fashioned."
- "If this woman is old-fashioned, in the age of the horseless carriage, she is like a horse with blinders on."
- By choosing to portray a woman as the subject of this criticism, there is the sexist subtext of the time: "Your husband might trade you in for a faster model."

Gadzooks, what a predicament!

While the content of the ad is politically incorrect by today's standards, the marketing technique was perfect. The product was unknown to its target market, so pitching features and benefits to people who weren't yet convinced that they needed the product at all would fall on deaf ears.

To attract buyers for the first time, marketers talked about a problem that they knew members of their target market identified with. They found that the most effective triggers were shame or guilt plus fear, uncertainty, and doubt (known as FUD). Old-school marketers call this the AIDA model (awareness, interest, desire, and action), which were featured in an explosive monologue delivered by actor Alec Baldwin in David Mamet's film adaptation of his Pulitzer Prize–and Tony-winning play *Glengarry Glen Ross* (New Line Cinema, 1992).

The first salvo of marketing for household consumer goods talked about a problem, made people *aware* that they had the problem, and sought to gain their *interest* in finding a solution—opening their mind opened the sale. This was called the *Door Opener*.

The second salvo came once prospects recognized that they had the problem. Either marketing or a sales agent reinforced the message of how bad the pain was, and suggested that the way to avoid that pain was to buy the product. This focused the consumer's *desire* on a solution, and a call to *action* was elicited after the consumer was convinced that one brand was better than another. This was called the *Door Closer*.

Door Openers and Door Closers were delivered in newspapers, magazines, and other publications, as well as on radio and television. Sometimes the function of a Door Closer was reinforced by salespeople at the point of sale in a showroom, on the telephone, on the doorstep, in the lounge room, or over the counter.

The third and final salvo came after prospects became customers. Marketing exposed customers to a different stream of advertisements that showed happy and successful people benefiting from the product, reinforcing what a wise decision it was to buy—and to keep buying over and over. This was called the *Revolving Door*.

This three-step marketing model (see Figure 2.2) worked like a dream for household consumer goods. Then companies started using it for marketing to other companies. Business-to-business (B2B) marketing was born.

The first to do so were companies selling close cousins of household consumer goods—those selling "office consumer goods," such as plain and carbon paper supplies, index cards, office furniture, adding machines, accounting services, cash registers, typewriters, and "office lithography" (the forerunners of today's document management and computing businesses, such as Xerox, 3M, and IBM). We believe it is

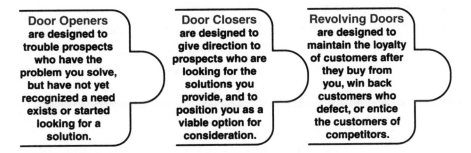

Figure 2.2 Classic Three-Step Marketing Model of the Early 1900s

no coincidence that these companies are remembered for having developed some of the world's first programmatic sales training.

For example, Xerox bought *Professional Selling Skills* from Pfizer and used it to train every one of its salespeople for many years, even after it was spun out as an independent training business in the 1980s (it is now owned by Achieve Global). Xerox also commissioned a large research project on selling skills in the 1970s, which provided the foundation for Neil Rackham and Huthwaite to develop *SPIN Selling*. Most of today's skills-based sales training can be traced back to Xerox, whose initiatives, in turn, can be traced back to the way consumer goods were marketed and sold in the early 1900s.

But by the mid-1900s, the wave of industrialization and mechanization had peaked. New products were still being invented, but only within product categories that were already familiar to customers. The negative overtones of the Door Opener's problem-based marketing were replaced by the positive messages of the Revolving Door. The Door Closer stage has since stayed with showroom or territory salespeople and, where possible, has been pushed to lower-cost channels such as call centers, distributors, and online commerce.

For the *marketing of consumer products to households*, this was the right approach to take. The retail game isn't about getting consumers to accept a new product category anymore (they aren't being invented as frequently as they used to be). It's about getting customers to defect from one brand and go to another, stay true to your brand, and buy more. People know what they need, and as long as their favorite brand is available or an alternative brand catches their attention, they will spend their money on that category when they have the need for it and the disposable income to afford it. Most consumer marketing therefore sells how strong, sexy, beautiful, fashionable, trendy, healthy, or wise a product will make you appear to yourself and to others, and then it's about being able to complete a transaction where and when a customer wants to buy.

Because consumer marketing had taken this route, business marketing followed. And this is where almost every company and almost every advertising agency in the world made a critical marketing gaffe.

Cutting back on problem-based marketing was entirely the wrong thing to do in B2B. Why? Because as a "collection of people" who come and go, companies are not as self-aware concerning their needs as individual consumers, who live permanently inside their own skin, are. What self-awareness companies do develop is lost every time a key officer leaves her job and a new person takes over.

Think of the last time you took over someone else's job and the quality of the handover you received, if any. Were you given a complete explanation of why things are done the way they are and where all the problems are? With the average tenure of sales directors being three years, it's not too great a stretch to conclude that they spend their first 12 months finding out what's broken, the next 12 months papering over the cracks, and the final 12 months shopping their CV for a new job. Knowledge leaves the organization. Problems remain unresolved, yet they still lurk in the background, affecting corporate performance.

This dynamism of personnel and lack of "corporate memory" is a key reason why companies need to be continually awakened to the fact that problems exist, and that your company has the solution to those problems. But advertising agencies stopped applying problem-based marketing to corporate clients' campaigns, universities stopped teaching it as part of the curriculum, and all the lemmings ran off the same cliff.

So while there are very bright and creative people running marketing departments, chances are that, through no fault of their own, their college classes taught them only generic marketing and missed the most important aspects of B2B demand creation through problem-based marketing, which ironically was the original foundation of *all marketing* at the end of the nineteenth century.

We were curious to see whether any university in the world taught a specific B2B marketing program that was materially different from the curriculum for retail and consumer marketing. A quick search engine poll using terms like "+B2B +marketing +school +curriculum" returned 18,000 hits. Then we refined our search to exclude words like "curriculum vitae," "résumé," and "consumer" (and any link to "junior," "middle," and "high" schools). Finally, we added "+problem" to our list (minus "problem solver" or "problem solving").

Our 18,000 hits immediately dropped to just 82, and within these, only one university's executive MBA program held the right content. In a haystack of 18,000 straws, we found one needle, and we found that one only because we knew what to look for. How do you think most high school graduates fare when they're choosing a marketing degree? How about those that skip college and learn on the job?

So it's really not surprising that when we ask marketing directors in B2B organizations to explain their marketing mix, we learn that they are *technically proficient* at segmentation, database scrubbing, and targeting, as well as in using a multichannel print, online, and digital media strategy. The names in the database are usually the right business contacts. And if their key performance indicators are to release X number of press releases to analysts and journalists per year, run Y number of conferences and events to achieve a minimum attendance goal, and pull Z number of leads from these conferences and trade shows, then most B2B marketing managers end their year feeling that they've done a pretty good job. And if they were working in consumer retail companies, they'd be right. But not if they're working in B2B.

Most people don't give this much thought because all through their career, marketing leads have been so-so, and they probably think that's just how it goes. You can tell if your marketing team is running a retail consumer goods strategy in your B2B market if it lacks answers to the following 10 simple questions:

1. What is the problem that our company solves better than our competitors do? What target market most has that problem?
2. What messages do we send that are designed to trouble prospects about the latent problem that they have (and that we solve)?

3. How many executives with latent needs will we discover this year and turn into leads? How long will it take?
4. How many leads will be handed to sales this year? Next quarter, the quarter after that, and next year?
5. How many of those leads won't give a first meeting?
6. How many executives who give a first meeting will progress to a proposal? How long does it take?
7. How many executives who are sent proposals are converted into contracts by sales? How long does it take?
8. What revenue and profit come from those contracts?
9. How are the executives who don't make it (from name to lead to first meeting to proposal to contract) followed up?
10. How many leads that don't buy on the first pass are reanimated through follow-up activities?

Could the marketing manager in your company answer all these questions? Maybe. As we've stated, it's our observation that most marketing managers are technically proficient but lacking in B2B strategy because they've never really been taught it, despite the way their textbooks were labeled. And to cut them some slack, how could they ever have been taught it when all the marketing theory taught in today's schools is based on the household consumer goods model, which dropped the concept of problem-based marketing half a century ago?

As a result, we see companies pumping out feel-good marketing about how happy their customers are, how solid their company is, how many awards the company is winning, how experienced its leaders are, and every detail about its product features and benefits. These attempts at marketing encourage existing customers to stay in the user community and give direction to prospects who have already identified what their problem is and are searching for a supplier.

But as with telephone directory advertising, these customers will find you only if their fingers do the walking. Marketing is trying to be seen where customers are looking, but it isn't doing much to create demand where it didn't exist before, and in many cases it's obliterating the salesperson's ability to engage with executives. Most important, those executives can form all the opinions they need (right or wrong) about you and your competitors by clicking their mouse.

So leads get created; some where customers have already been educated by your Web site and some where they've already been educated by your competitors. If a prospect is breathing and shows a pulse, we put that prospect in our pipeline to keep the sales manager off our back. After all, we have a quota for new leads to fill, and we might get lucky. Even a blind squirrel finds a nut now and then.

But all salespeople know that there's a lot of fiction in their forecasts. It's the elephant in the living room that nobody wants to acknowledge. And until we get better-quality leads from marketing, we're loath to cull the dead and weak leads because the alternative is to go prospecting—and we all know how much most salespeople enjoy that slice of heaven. Forecasts swell with all manner of fiction, multiplied by every salesperson in the field, multiplied by every week of the year.

Is it any wonder that a recent Ernst & Young study of 1,100 companies found that three-month forecasts are generally more than 40 percent wrong? Many deals simply should not be on the forecast in the first place because they have no hope of turning into anything but a drain on the salesperson's time as he offers "free education" to a person who may show some curiosity, but who has no need or intention of buying.

Pipelines bloated with phantom sales opportunities are the bane of every sales manager's end-of-month forecast. Many managers will argue that their forecasts are more accurate than this, and that orders come in near the size and the date originally indicated. We hope they're right.

Of course, we also hope that before they beat their chests too hard, they inspect the deals that are sitting fallow in the pipeline for longer than the average time it should take to close them (these may be dead already), or the "strategic deals" that stay in the forecast for multiple years just in case hope really *is* a strategy. The truth is, there's only so much lipstick you can put on this pig.

Forecasts are littered with the debris of deals that have already foundered or are about to, and this number is in direct proportion to the quality of the leads provided by marketing, the courage of the sales force to qualify out, and the rigor of inspection by the sales manager.

To the heads of marketing departments goes this clarion call:

> Wake up if you thought that marketing was about being creative and winning design awards. It's about making money. Money! B2B marketing should be a hard science of ratios, revenue, and ROI, not the soft refuge of breakfasts and brochures that many have allowed it to become. Because the acid test of your contribution is this: if your CEO spun your department out and made your contract dependent on your showing a quantifiable impact on closed sales revenue in the next six months, could you measure that, or would you be out of a job? Because if you would be then, shouldn't you be now?

And to CEOs who have no real idea what marketing does, and so use it as their first target when times get tough and they need to slash budgets:

> Isn't it about time you applied the same rigor of process and measurement as you do in other mission-critical parts of the business? Because in good times and bad, it's marketing that primes the pump and sales that pulls the water. If leads aren't coming in the door, everything stops. If the leads given to the sales force are weak, everything stops. If sales managers aren't inspecting the detail, everything stops. And if sales aren't

happening, cash flow stops. Never thought of sales and marketing as mission-critical? Try running your business without cash. Even annuity businesses like accounting, tax agents, and software licensors know better than to rely on past deeds to pay tomorrow's bills. Don't allow sales and marketing to remain the last bastion of dark arts in your company. If you want a business you can predict and scale, then fix your marketing strategy and fix your sales execution. Not being able to certify either as a transparent part of your revenue growth strategy should be grounds for immediate dismissal in this post-Enron age.

So *Selling to the C-Suite* really begins with the tenet that if marketers continue to flood the Internet with free information about their company and its products, they're contributing to the "democratization of information" that pushes salespeople down to the level of Commodity Suppliers instead of Trusted Advisors.

With this sobering thought in mind, we declare B2B marketing to be fundamentally broken in most companies around the world. Our opinion is developed from three sources.

First, we listened to salespeople—the real customers of a marketing unit. Overwhelmingly, hundreds of thousands of the sales reps we've met and trained around the world tell us that many of the leads they receive from promotions, trade shows, and other campaigns are far from qualified when they're handed over by marketing. Salespeople have come to regard marketing teams as brand police who patrol the beat of breakfasts and brochures, but rarely produce anything that leads to revenue. It's a harsh view, but it's not undeserved.

Second, we listened to marketers themselves, who volunteer that they don't really know how their work affects revenue. They told us that prospects' business cards collected at trade shows and seminars are offered out of politeness or a desire to win the door prize. It's the same with names that pop out of banner ads and telemarketing blitzes: they're not "hot leads" by any stretch of the imagination. We also heard marketers express concern that in the absence of anything better to work with, they were measuring performance using metrics taken from retail marketing.

Third, we did hard research into this topic. The 2007 CSO Insights study on sales optimization and the 2007 Ernst & Young research into the drivers of sustainable revenue growth reveal that across more than 2,400 companies surveyed, for every 100 prospects that marketing finds, an average of only 2.3 progress to a contract with sales. Anyone with a Six Sigma background should be horrified at this 97.7 percent failure rate! Updates to these studies in 2008 are even more troubling, suggesting that for every 111 prospects found by marketing, only 1 progressed all the way to a sales contract—a 99.1 percent failure rate. We are prepared to concede that the financial recession in 2008 may explain such a dramatic drop in a single year. However, the trend across the entire five-year period cannot be ignored; it is conclusive and should serve as a wake-up call to anyone in the sales and marketing profession.

It's commonplace to hear a CEO say: "I know half my marketing budget is being wasted; I just don't know which half!" So what is missing is a process that aligns sales and marketing with how the firm's customers buy, a clear delineation of responsibility for delivering certain information to those customers, and measures to tell if each department is producing enough throughput of leads and sales to achieve the company's revenue goals.

In a September 2000 interview with SalesLobby.com, Neil Rackham (author of *SPIN Selling* in 1988 and coauthor of *Rethinking the Sales Force* in 1999) commented on the effect the Internet had on traditional selling models, and suggested what lay in store:

Information-based selling, the talking brochure selling, is just going to die out because you can't afford it when it's more costly and less convenient; and until the Internet came along you had to have it because you had no alternative. We think of the Internet sometimes as a selling medium, but in fact it's a buying medium. Most business-to-business commerce on the Internet is initiated by the buyer, not the seller. Salespeople of the future have to actually create value, not communicate value. So, another way to put this is that the salesperson in the future has to make the kind of sales calls where the customer would pull out a checkbook and write a check for the call because it was so valuable. In the future, they're going to have to do that in every call. We've done surveys where we've asked customers, have you ever had a salesperson call on you where you really would have pulled out a checkbook and written them a personal check for a sales call? To those that said yes, we said, tell us about it. The most common single factor in what they described is that this salesperson *"changed the way I thought about my problems. I did something very differently as a result of talking to them."* Now, if you're going to do that with your customers, you've got to be much more challenging, you've got to be able to come in as business equals, you've got to focus on the problem and not on the product.[1]

When marketing becomes a barrier to salespeople having these value-creation discussions with executives, it's not only a matter of rethinking the sales force but of rethinking sales and marketing from the ground up. The emerging best practice is to focus both departments on what's called the "Buyer's Journey," a term first coined by Hugh Macfarlane in his book *The Leaky Funnel*. Have both departments concentrate on their roles of creating demand (marketing) and then creating value (sales) in a way that leads the buyer down a cognitive journey of discovery and decision.

This book isn't about the role of marketing. But we feel that this issue is of critical importance to the topic of selling at the executive level. For salespeople to have a chance at building and maintaining

C-level relationships, B2B marketing on the Internet must stop robbing salespeople of the opportunity to provide insight to the executive's thought process.

A few enlightened companies have awakened and decided to solve the problem. They use the Internet to tease prospects through the Buyer's Journey until they beat a path to the seller's door. Using this model, the first task of marketing is to educate buyers on the fact that they have a problem. All direct mail, call center activity, events, and permission-based e-mailing focus on the customers' most pressing problems to help them say: "Hey, I have that symptom, and I understand its implications; I'm now aware, troubled, and ready to be sold to." This is what Michael Bosworth described in his book *Solution Selling* (McGraw-Hill, 1995) as turning a customer with a latent pain into a customer with an active pain through a system of "hurt and rescue." A customer with a latent pain will spend time, but only a customer with an active pain will spend money.

So these prospects move from having a latent or chronic pain that they've learned to live with or never even recognized to feeling agitated about a pain that they now want to fix. Achieving this cognitive transformation doesn't happen overnight, which is why the latest generation of marketers designs campaigns that hit buyers between the eyes with their problem again and again and again until they wake up. White papers, research studies, and panel breakfasts prove to be effective methods for achieving this goal, with each exchange adding value to the prospect's thought process at the same time as it captures data on the prospect and her situation.

As reinforcement, marketing's next task is to optimize the company's hits on search engines to make it appear to be a credible provider in the right category, and to ensure that the company's Web site is informative without stealing the thunder from sales. If you've ever downloaded a file from a Web site and been asked to answer several survey questions in return, you've participated in this form of marketing. Over time, as you respond in certain ways and return to the Web site for updates, the seller organization amasses high-quality profile data that identifies whether you fit its target market and what your biggest issues are.

With the assistance of behavioral lead-scoring software, these companies also know exactly when a prospect is ready to meet a salesperson—who can now have that discussion armed with a highly accurate profile of the buyer's situation, needs, and wants. Of course, once they have awakened to their pain, buyers won't wait for the salesperson to call. But if the process is done correctly, that call *will* come at about the same time that the buyer starts actively pinging the Internet to see who can help solve the problem he now recognizes that he has (where, hopefully, he will find your problem-based Web site talking about his world, not yours). To an executive, the salesperson's call appears to be a serendipitous coincidence. But it's really the result of having adopted good marketing science, process, and measurement. This "new" field of problem-based marketing campaign management is a rediscovery of the original marketing science, and it drives Internet-savvy executives to ask questions of a higher order than their price-conscious subordinates will, in turn preserving a role for salespeople to contribute to the Buyer's Journey early.

We won't provide a full treatise on this topic here, as there are whole books devoted to the subject; the best we've seen are *The Buck Starts Here*, by Mary and Michael Molloy (Thomson Executive, 1996), *The Leaky Funnel*, by Hugh Macfarlane (Mathmarketing, 2004), and Robert J. Schmonsees's *Escaping the Black Hole* (Southwestern Educational Press, 2005). We recommend that every chief sales officer, chief marketing officer, and CEO read these books and ponder the implications of being left behind in the current wave of marketing automation and transformation. A whole software industry supports this new science, led by brands like Eloqua,[2] vTrenz,[3] and others.

If you're a senior executive, consider this your wake-up call to get your hands around this issue. If you're a salesperson who wants a future, get your executives involved in changing the way marketing creates qualified leads. Give them a copy of this book! Buying has already changed. If marketing and sales are to catch up, there's no time to lose. When you get questionable prospects from marketing and turn them into bona fide buyers, and when Web sites are redesigned to give away less of the information that salespeople should be delivering in person, your company will redefine the sales force as a relevant player at the C-suite.

The only remaining part of the puzzle is for salespeople to learn the latest approaches for gaining access to executives and creating value at the C-suite. This dimension of sales execution is what the rest of this book is about.

Chapter Summary

Let's summarize what we've discussed in this chapter by looking at the three key messages:

1. *Executives with an active need have already accessed the Internet.*

   When executives recognize a need, they start their own research by talking to people whose opinions they value and by doing their own detective work on the Internet. If they use a search engine to find the problem they have, they probably won't find most of the companies addressing it because most companies' Web sites use sales language (product), not buying language (problem). If they find the right product categories to look at, executives will quickly become expert enough on your company and your competitors to eliminate the need to meet with you for information. They will usually set the vision for a project and then delegate the management of vendors to someone at a lower level.

2. *Executives with a latent need aren't looking for you . . . yet.*
   Roughly two-thirds of a target market may be unaware that alternatives to the way they do business today exist. They remain untroubled by current or impending problems because those problems are simply not front-of-mind. If you help an executive see that she has a problem and she becomes troubled by it, you are on the scene at the origin of her thought process, and that involvement implies that you may have the answers she needs. More than half the sales opportunities where demand is created in this way do not go to competitive tender. Of those that

do go to tender, more than half are won by the first company to engage the executive on these issues, even if the executive delegates vendor management to lower levels of the organization.

3. *Too many Web sites steal the thunder from salespeople.* On many Web sites, details about a company's offerings and its thought leadership are given away for free, without capturing any information about the visitor. When executives have such a free buffet, they may not feel a need to meet a salesperson. The best practice is to pull executives to dynamic personalized URLs (PURLs) that discuss the problem they have and offer ideas in return for information about their business priorities, and to hand the lead to sales only after the prospect has reached a minimum score that indicates that he fits your target market, recognizes that he has the problem you solve, and wants to talk.

Chapter 3

Understanding What Executives Want

Understanding what motivates senior executives requires a keen understanding of the company's key business issues, including the business drivers that are creating the need for change and the initiatives the company has put in place to address those drivers. These issues may have a different impact on each senior executive in the client organization—mostly depending on the executive's specific function and role. In some cases, this information is easy to obtain (simply by reading the President's Letter in a recent annual report, for example), but in other cases, it may require a substantial amount of research before your critical call on the client executive.

In any case, executives expect salespeople to be prepared and to have a basic knowledge of the key issues facing them—before you meet with them. They don't expect to have to educate you on information that can be readily obtained, either from a public source (like the Internet) or from lower-level executives in the organization, whom they will presume you have already met.

Be aware of your client's internal or external business drivers. Any of these could create the need for change if it is deemed important enough to assign people, money, and time to it. This is where sales opportunities first get forged. You can learn about these pressures by talking to the customer and doing your own research. This tells you the customer's language and helps you talk like an insider. It also helps you put in context how your products and services will allow the company to do something better, faster, or easier than the approach the company is presently taking, which is the only reason an executive will buy from you. Explaining the executive's perspective on how you can do this effectively is what this chapter is all about.

HOW TO DO HIGHLY EFFECTIVE RESEARCH

Doing the legwork to fully understand an executive's needs is the foundation for evolving into a Trusted Advisor salesperson, yet many salespeople we work with confess that this is a very difficult thing to do on a regular basis.

It seems a challenge to find the time to read industry magazines or business periodicals, profile the client's current affairs on the Internet, or learn the client's issues and jargon at symposiums and conferences. Yet if you aspire to create value for your customers as a Trusted Advisor and engage their executives early in the buying cycle, this is the price for admission. Immersing yourself in your customers' world will help you rise above the herd and be recognized as a real player, as well as a real contributor to their success.

A few hours a week is all it takes to brush up on the latest events in your customers' industries. Back in the late 1980s, it seemed that every third salesperson carried a Franklin Planner or Day-Timer. These organized souls took the responsibility for taking time out of their busy schedules and planning their business with a cultish zeal. Mantras like "plan the work and work the plan" or "failing to plan is planning to fail" were chunks of coal to a generation intent on making its own diamonds. There was something at once therapeutic, tactile, and empowering in penciling "planning time" into the schedule to make a plan, do it, measure it, and then plan all over again.

With so much noise competing for our attention today, there's an argument that there's no time for this level of detailed planning anymore and that Outlook and Notes Calendar entries are adequate. On the other hand, there's an argument that in the face of so much distraction, there's never been a greater need for planning. One thing is certain: if you don't plan to take the time to stay current on your customers and prospects, the information won't pop into your head by itself.

Top salespeople we have met around the world always do four things on a regular basis to stay on top of their customers' changing world. They know that they need to "go to school" on their prospects and key accounts or risk becoming irrelevant. Here's what they do.

1. Get Into the Game

Salespeople whose careers started in the past 20 years of economic growth around the world have never really faced a difficult market. Those older sages who remember the decimation of the mid-1970s and 1980s recessions know that there comes a time when the phone stops ringing and tenders dry up. When the 2008 stock market and housing bubbles started to falter in many nations, it was a reminder that difficult times can always return, and that when they do, a typical reaction for buyers is to slash spending.

So salespeople everywhere need to decide to truly get into the game of being rainmakers and not wait for customers to approach them. This is to say: "I will maximize my value to my customer executives this year by learning all I can about them, their company, their competitors, and their industries, and bringing them new ideas that they will then pay me to implement. The more I mean to them, the more they will mean to me."

Selling is not a spectator sport. Get into the game.

2. Work Backward

This is the "if you can see it, you can be it" psych-up used by sports professionals at the start of any grueling training regime. Dynamic modeling involves visualizing where you want to be, then planning backward those things that you must put in place to make it a reality. Some people also call this regression planning.

If your vision is to create value for executives, it stands to reason that you must first anticipate where your customers want to go and what they want to achieve, then work backward from those outcomes to piece together several ways in which your company can help them achieve those goals. When you begin with the customer's destination and work backward to find the appropriate solution, you will typically research and uncover a range of useful information that even people in the executive's own company haven't thought of. That's valuable.

3. Adopt a Routine

One of the behaviors observed in Generation X workers (now in senior sales or management roles) and Generation Y workers (now starting to enter the sales profession) is that having been raised in the era of Everything Now (drive-through food, instant messaging, broadband downloads, and fast-track career paths), they have a tendency to dismiss activities whose results are not immediately visible, and leave those boring tasks for someone else to complete. Similarly, some old sales dogs who have worked in a territory for a long time may feel that they know what's going on by osmosis. All we'll say here is that researching your customer is a matter of personal accountability. If you don't schedule a *sacrosanct* time each week to sit down and study your customers, nobody else will step in and do it for you. Except maybe your competitors.

4. Ask Lots of Questions

We once heard an area sales manager coach his team as follows: "An executive is someone who has no time to listen to you but has all day to talk to you." Add to that the wisdom of all lawyers: "Never ask a question you don't already know the answer to," and you learn that when you research your customers and understand their hot spots, you are equipping yourself to open up the conversations that an executive most wants to have. Let the executive talk. Understand her point of view. Then she'll eventually turn the discussion to understanding you, like, "So what do you do and how can you help me?" Ka-ching!

Understand the customer. Ask questions based on your research so that you can lead the discussion where you want it to go. This will get you credit for having done your homework on the client organization before meeting the executive. Ask other questions to find out the things that only the executive can tell you. The customer will respond in kind by asking to understand you better. When that happens, you're not selling; he's buying. It makes all the difference in the world.

As an aid to researching customers and prospects, we include a step-by-step "Guide to Customer Research" in Appendix 1 of this book. It's already been road-tested by thousands of salespeople who have attended our workshops, and it offers practical advice on using the Internet and other resources to stay abreast of customer developments.

Gaining a deep understanding of an executive's issues, pressures, and drivers helps you anticipate that executive's future requirements and how the products and services that you provide may be relevant. Competitive salespeople use this information in discussions to explore potential needs and to send a signal that they can add business value. Demystifying the C-suite is all about doing your homework.

Here's what one sales professional shared about this topic:

Senior-level executives are very busy, and they want some assurance that meeting with you is worth their time. It's like a job interview. A candidate needs to show relevant experience on her CV or résumé and come to the interview able to talk to the issues that are important to the employer. You can't know what those issues are unless you do your homework. For salespeople, every sales call is a job interview—we're serial job hunters! When I'm preparing for an executive sales call, I try to determine the specific business value I might put on the table. I look at the customer's Web site and Google phrases like "strategy" and "press release" connected to the company, and the names of the top executives associated with the company's competitors. Sometimes I'll add the names of the company's biggest customers to see what they're doing in the market and if my prospect is (or should be) proactive about serving those needs. I also refine those searches to show only the past three to six months so that what I read about is still current. It's amazing how many investor presentations, analyst reports, or journalist reviews you can find. This tells me the customer's language, his strategy, and what his rivals are doing. This type of research might take an hour or two, but that's the discipline you need to truly be ready for the hour in front of the executive. So when my competitors meet the same executive and ask, "What are your top three business objectives?" I can be in there saying, "I understand your top three business objectives are X, Y, and Z; which one is most important to you and why?" You see the difference? I'm able to show that I did my homework and then get something the Internet can't always give me—the executive's insight! These are the discussions that make sales, and why doing your homework is the best preparation for demystifying the C-suite.

We're big fans of this type of preparation. But having run thousands of sales coaching sessions over the years, we're still amazed at how many salespeople fail to do it.

Case in point: while doing the final edit of this book, an invitation came in to help a sales team review its plan for a million-dollar deal. The team sold business analytics, and the prospect was a leading cable TV brand that wanted to segment its customers better.

We reviewed the sales team's opportunity plan, and it was clear that the team members enjoyed strong mentor-style relationships with a few mid-level managers in the prospect's database marketing department, where the product would be installed. But despite knowing these people, the sales team wasn't learning enough about them, nor were its members doing research on their prospect's business. Until the team lifted its sale above the product pitch and started focusing on the prospect's larger world, all its firm could ever be was a product vendor.

So before the coaching call, we invested two hours on Google. We learned that the prospect had recently shuffled its executive managers around. We wrote this down. We did background searches on each of these executives, and found that some of them had presented papers at recent conferences or been cited in magazines talking about issues that were important to them. We wrote this down. Then we searched for links between the prospect's company and the sales team's competitors, and we found every past press release that cited sales made into that company by those competitors, the reasons for those sales, and the customer executive who made the decision to buy (for this we extended our search parameters to a three-year period of time). And we wrote down what we found.

We learned that the CIO had inherited the role from one of the company's founders, who, three years before, had signed a multimillion-dollar deal with the main competitor of the team we were coaching. Would the new CIO reverse a decision made by the family that still controlled the company? Unlikely. Unless this sales team could find a reason to meet with other executives of at least equal rank or influence and build a support base with them, it could be facing a brick wall.

A few more clicks of our mouse and we read that the prospect had recently raised billions of dollars to buy the company's shares back from investors and delist it from the stock market to be a private company again. We wrote this down. The prospect had just acquired a major newspaper with readers in the same geographic area as the parent company's cable TV customers. We wrote this down. It was rolling out a Wi-Fi network and adding several new high-definition channels to its cable and satellite packages. We wrote this down.

The board was clearly intent on giving its customers greater breadth of content, while at the same time owning the multiple media distribution channels needed to deliver that content. It was transforming the company into a media powerhouse, cross-pollinating online and print entertainment, information, and advertising. To do that effectively, it would need to promote the right package to the right customers at the right time—the sort of capability you get from good business analytics software.

When we dialed into the sales team for our coaching call, we opened with a few questions like: "Why does the database marketing team need your product?" and "Is anything happening at a business level that might be driving this at the technical level?" The members of the sales team reported a few ideas that focused on the features and functions of their product, but they didn't see the bigger picture. After we shared what we had uncovered, there was stunned silence, then a murmur of hope. Half an hour later, the team members had created a whole new plan of attack that was on message and relevant to what this prospect was trying to achieve. And at last, *they* wrote it down.

With a little bit of homework, they now understood the context of the sale and were better prepared than ever to add value to their customer's thought process. And the team's sales manager was reminded of how important it is to step back from the sale and try to understand the bigger picture.

So how do you understand those drivers that shape an executive's decision process?

THE DRIVERS OF EXECUTIVE DECISION MAKING

Figure 3.1 depicts the drivers that are most likely to be behind your customer's thought process when it comes to making investments with suppliers.

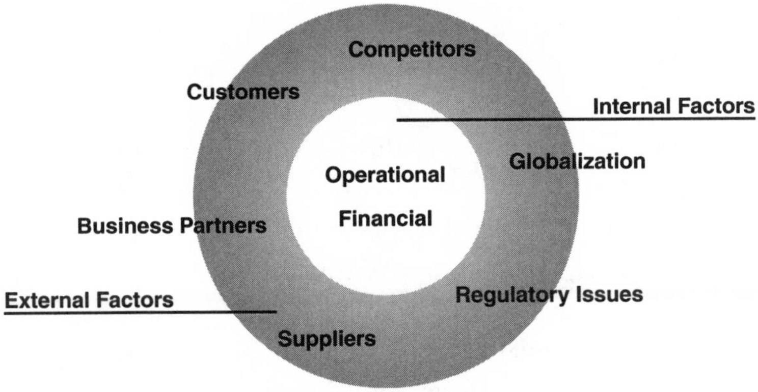

Figure 3.1 Drivers of Executive Decision Making

Think of the image as a cross section of an arm that shows the white "bone" in the center, surrounded by the "muscles." In this visual analogy, we'll say that the bone represents internal factors that provide stability to a company, typified by operational and financial resources such as money, talent, infrastructure, procedures, culture, systems, and measurement, all of which are used to underpin performance.

Continuing our visual analogy, a company's bones are connected to the outside world through muscles that affect and in turn are affected by six different external factors: the supply chain drivers of *suppliers*, *business partners*, and *customers*, and the marketplace drivers of *competitors*, *globalization*, and *regulatory issues* (we've included a business issues worksheet to help you profile these drivers in Appendix 2 of this book).

Let's examine what each of the eight drivers means to you as a salesperson.

Financial Drivers

Every executive is under financial pressure to perform. At the most basic level, executives must do one of two things to produce a profit: increase revenue or reduce costs. For salespeople to build business value for an executive who is pressured by financial drivers, they must ultimately help the executive move the needle on either profit or cost, and do so in a way that's consistent with how her industry measures success.

For example, in the airline industry, you'll get on the executive's radar if you're articulate about the drivers that are specific to airlines, such as load factor, a variable planning horizon, high seasonality, fierce competition, excessive government intervention, high fixed costs, and low margins (while the airline industry generates billions of dollars, it has a cumulative profit margin of less than 1 percent).[1] Show how your solution affects these financial or industry drivers, and you'll get the executive's attention.

When you're selling to a bank, different drivers are of interest: organic growth, maintaining customer loyalty, increasing customer transactions, risk management, reducing fraud and bad debts, consolidating and upgrading infrastructure, shifting from bricks (branches) to clicks (online banking), industry reform and regulation, merchant alliances, and so on.

One caveat: when you're using the customer's industry jargon, be sure you really understand how the customer uses it in context. We once observed a telecom salesperson in steamy Jakarta present to the CIO of a bank, who responded favorably to the value of *asynchronous transfer mode* (ATM) on his wide area network. In the afternoon this rep made the same pitch to the bank's vice president of retail banking. After 30 minutes hearing about "ATM this" and "ATM that," the vice president realized that the rep had no clue about his business and playfully gave the salesperson a verbal agreement to buy 500 new ATMs at a price he felt was too good to pass up—then he told the rep he expected *automated teller machines* to bolt onto the outside of his banks, not the asynchronous transfer mode software that comes on a CD! As the rep woke up to his error, this executive stood up and opened the door, ending the meeting. On the way to the elevator, this vice president made small talk and asked the salesperson, "How do you think SOX will affect us?" He was referring to the Sarbanes-Oxley legislation, which requires SEC-registered entities to adopt corporate accounting controls. The sandal-wearing salesperson demonstrated an appalling lack of appreciation of the banking industry by replying, "In this heat I think socks would make our feet too hot. I never wear them." He was never invited back.

The jargon a company uses to talk about its business is like a tribal language. As a rule, it's unwise to throw those labels around hoping to make an impression unless you truly understand their interpretations and implications. To cite an old Spanish proverb: "It is better to stay silent and conceal one's knowledge than to speak and reveal one's ignorance."

Operational Drivers

Executives concern themselves with trying to determine how to improve the internal organization and affect the financial return based on that improvement. At the most basic level, executives are concerned about having the right strategy, taking advantage of the latest approaches, and having the right people, processes, and technologies to execute that strategy.

One executive in our study looks to salespeople as gateways for "expertise we don't have, coupled with experience for producing this type of capability."

Look at how you can help executives do a better job of making, quality controlling, selling, and delivering their business plan. All of these will be affected by the effectiveness (doing the right things) and efficiencies (doing things right) in the operation.

Supplier Drivers

As a result of Six Sigma, Total Quality Management, and Supply Chain Reengineering, large companies are routinely reducing the number of suppliers they buy materials and services from in the hope that buying more from a smaller pool of suppliers creates less complexity, simpler accounting, and improved buying power.

If you are an executive in a company that is on the *selling side* of the supply chain, your concern is first about winning the contract, then about preserving quality and margins with buyers who know how important their trade is to you and will try to reduce your price at every contract renewal. If you aggregate parts of your offering from different locations, you will obsess over the smallest fluctuations in foreign exchange rates, gasoline prices, labor costs, political policy, and even how changes in the weather might interrupt your just-in-time manufacturing and supply logistics. Buying too much raw material, having too many pallets aging in warehouses and on wharves, or losing too many crates in transit equates to poor Supply Chain

Management. Finding the right balance is something you want to achieve.

If you are an executive on the *buying side* of the supply chain, your concern is with the reliability of supply, quality, economies of scale, inventory turnover, shrinkage through loss or theft, warehousing and distribution technologies, demand forecasting, and many of the same issues that trouble executives on the selling side of the supply chain. There's very much a level of interdependence between the buyer and the seller, so approaches to real-time data sharing, shared infrastructure, and shared risk management remain compelling issues to discuss, especially when a salesperson can cogently explain how any of his company's solutions in these areas can do the job faster, better, or with less risk than the way the executive does it today.

Business Partner Drivers

At times, new alliances are created between former competitors in order to thwart a competitor they share in common, as advised by the Arabian proverb: "The enemy of my enemy is my friend." Your customers may even now be evaluating their business partner relationships in light of changing business environments. This represents another opportunity to create value by demonstrating an understanding of the customer's pressures and offering solutions by orchestrating relevant introductions to your company's network of people, partners, and affiliates who have value to add. Solutions are sometimes more about the relationships you help broker than about the product or service you sell.

If you were the executive you're selling to, your thoughts might regularly turn to pondering how to find new business partners, ensuring that they are the right fit, keeping them informed and educated, testing the quality of what they do and its effect on your brand, avoiding channel conflict, and making the relationship profitable. So put yourself in the executive's shoes. Explore how she does these things today, and you may see ways in which your company can make a positive difference. The executive will listen.

Customer Drivers

Maintaining and growing their existing customer base, creating and enhancing loyalty, and delivering value are of prime importance to most executives. But how do you target the right customers? How do you anticipate their needs? How do you develop new products that will be ready when the market starts to demand them? How can you tell which customers are your best ones? How can you keep your best customers loyal? How do you balance your business so that it's not overly dependent on a small list of customers who do most of the spending? As a salesperson, if you can demonstrate how your product or service can add value in these areas, you will be seen as a resource who can help create a competitive advantage, and executives will want to talk to you if they recognize that they have a problem in this area.

According to one account manager who sells to the financial services industry:

> You have to first understand the client's business and the demands on that business. We talk about the company's unique situations. For example, some brokerage houses have investment tools that are out of date after a few days. How do you help them maximize their profitability during that time? How do you let brokers know who is calling in and what his portfolio looks like so that they can leverage that knowledge? These are the types of problems we discuss with executives in an effort to become involved in setting the future direction.

Competitor Drivers

Competitors are another significant source of pressure for the executive. The traditional direct competitors are easy to identify, but nontraditional ones are more difficult to spot. For example, a few years ago, who could see that local telephone carriers would become cable TV businesses? Who saw that UK supermarkets like Tesco and clothing chains like Marks & Spencer would get into financial services and communications by offering their retail customers personal loans, insurance, Internet connections, and mobile phone services?

While executives immerse themselves in their own company affairs, the fact that you sell to many companies places you in a unique position to offer something those executives are always looking for: insight into marketplace trends. So share your ideas and help them see beyond their silo walls to how other companies are solving the same competitor drivers they face.

Globalization Drivers

Globalization affects executives in a variety of ways. As they face competition from cheaper labor and production abroad, they risk losing market share. Consequently, to remain competitive, they must either drive cost out of their domestic infrastructure or outsource production and services to low-cost offshore providers. Either course of action creates risk as well as opportunity. How do they find the right production and distribution partners? How do they drive risk out of an extended supply chain and hedge for multiple currencies? How do they recruit and keep the right people? How will customers in different countries enjoy a uniform customer experience? How will staff members in different countries experience a consistent company culture that still resonates locally? If globalization means closing domestic factories, how will they manage labor laws, public relations, and finances? Do they have products that appeal to multiple markets? Does their brand play correctly when translated into other languages?

Ford faced this challenge when it discovered that Pinto translated as "young chicken" in Portuguese. Chevrolet's Nova translated as "it doesn't go" in Spanish. When Coca-Cola launched in China, it found that the phonetically similar name "*Koukou-kole*" translated as "happiness in the mouth," but only after the failure of the first name it tried: "*Kekou-kela*," which means "female horse stuffed with wax."

Helping executives anticipate and navigate these issues is a tremendously valuable contribution, but to do so, you need to have studied the company's situation and weighed the company's options as judiciously as though you were on its board—that's the value executives are looking for.

Regulatory Drivers

In response to the corporate scandals that have filled the headlines in the past decade, governments, industry regulators, and shareholders are demanding greater accountability and transparency from corporations. Companies must operate under new regulations designed to maintain stability in financial markets that are already under pressure, and to protect shareholder interests by restoring investor confidence.

The regulatory drivers that keep executives awake at night include financial accounting compliance, workplace safety, labor laws, equal opportunity, environmental emissions and carbon credits, anti-money laundering, and international tax rules.

To illustrate how personal accountability is being policed, ex-WorldCom CEO Bernard Ebbers and former Enron CEO Jeff Skilling both received 25 years in prison for their personal complicity in their companies' failure to comply with the law. This is serious stuff! From Australia to Zimbabwe, you can Google the phrase "corporate scandal" and find thousands of articles that serve as cautionary tales.

Research conducted by PR firm Weber Shandwick reports that the number of CEOs ousted against their will increased dramatically in 2007 compared to 2006. In North America, 37 percent of CEOs were fired in 2007 compared to 17 percent in 2006. In Europe that number was 32 percent, and in Asia Pacific it was 24 percent.[2] These findings were consistent with separate studies by *Forbes*[3] and Booz Allen Hamilton.[4]

According to the "CEO Stick Rate Report" released by the executive recruitment firm CT Partners, the intense scrutiny and accountability required by Sarbanes-Oxley regulations has definitely taken its toll on CEO tenure since 2002: "We found a 91.3% increase in the number of Fortune 100 CEO departures in the five years following Sarbanes-Oxley in 2002 compared to the five years prior."[5]

If you have a solution that helps executives stay compliant with regulations and stay out of jail, and if you can demonstrate how this solution will work in the context of their business today, you'll unlock the C-suite every time.

In most sales situations, if you ask questions about and do research on the ways in which these six external drivers affect your prospect, it will serve as a trail of bread crumbs to the people inside the company who are most affected by those drivers—those with the most to gain or most to lose. Then, as you set up meetings with these people, ask how the external drivers affect their internal operational and financial "bones." Do the drivers create opportunities or threats? How does the company plan to flex its corporate "muscles" to respond? What is the executives' sense of urgency and priority? Then show how you can help.

If you don't research these issues, you won't be able to talk about them. This leaves you at Stage 1 of sales proficiency, where any attempt to meet the executives in a medium-size or large company will be perceived as an interruption. By taking the time to understand what's going on in your customer's world and forming your own opinions, you're equipped to be a Stage 2 salesperson, one who is more likely to be respected for your intent of making a contribution. Developing into a Stage 3 or Stage 4 salesperson is then a matter of practice and experience.

Of course, beyond their industry, company, and personal drivers are the issues that generally affect CXOs because of the office they

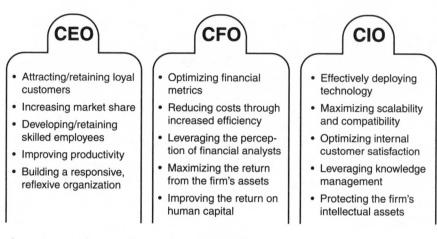

Figure 3.2 Role-Specific Issues Affecting Each CXO

hold (see Figure 3.2). These formal areas of accountability are unavoidable because they come with the job.

You can generally be confident that when you have studied the drivers affecting the executive's world, connecting them to executives' role-specific issues will give context to the discussion and serve as an additional framework for positioning why your products are relevant to them.

Chapter Summary

Let's summarize what we've discussed in this chapter by looking at the three key messages:

1. *Understand what motivates the executive.*

   Talk to the people who worked the account before you. Ransack the search engines. Look online for the executive's name as a speaker, conference delegate, or named source in a press release. See what issues she has risked her reputation on. Seek to understand how she made similar decisions in the past on the same subject or for contracts of a similar scope and size. If the executive is new to the role or is using it as a stepping-stone to better things, try to learn what triggers her interest and commitment. Is it purely a business outcome? Are there personal aspirations that need to be met? Is it about profits or people or position or power? If she's going to retire soon, find out what she wants to be remembered for, then help her get it. The point is, as the saying goes: "You can't sell John Smith what John Smith buys until you see through John Smith's eyes."

2. *Get into the game.*

   To stand out from a throng of me-too vendors, you must demonstrate your ability to be a business resource. This means doing more than parroting jargon in the hope that you'll sound the part. You need to know the specific business drivers that are motivating the executive's vision, and be prepared to explore these and offer opinions and insights so that the contribution of your product or service can be put in context. In this way it will be clear that you have value to add that the executive wouldn't gain without a vendor or can't gain from one of your competitors. In other words, you have value that can be clearly differentiated from the status quo *and* from other suppliers. If you got into the profession of business-to-business sales in an age where the fax machine spat out orders all day and times were good, or if your company brand and product quality drove sales to your door, you can be excused for never having mastered these skills and even being skeptical of the need for them. But how's that fax machine been performing for you lately? Don't make the mistake of denying the need for personal change, or you'll be wonderfully equipped . . . for a world that no longer exists.

3. *Right message, right audience.*
   No executive will spend money that he doesn't have to. His golden handshake depends on the profit and the share price achieved on his watch, so saving money—not spending it—will be a reflex for many, especially for those with a conservative accounting background who know that profit is made by increasing income or decreasing costs, with the lowest-risk action being to slash costs, delay expenditures, and cut heads. So if you're selling an idea for improving efficiency to conservative executives, frame your argument in terms of time, money, and saved resources. If you're selling an idea for raising quality to pragmatic executives, explain the quantitative and qualitative benefits of doing so. If you're selling an idea that helps your customer make

more money, be sure you have the right audience of visionary or innovative executives. The right message will fall flat with the wrong audience. This is why it's so important to do your homework not only on the business issues, but on the people you're selling to as well.

How to Gain
Access to the
Executive Level

Gaining a first meeting with senior-level executives is relatively straightforward for most professional salespeople with a bit of preparation and personal chutzpah. However, gaining return access to those same executives again and again is the real art. Executives don't waste time with people who add no value. More challenging still is building the type of trusted relationship where the executive will call you to discuss issues that are unrelated to anything you might be selling, but that are on her mind and that she hopes you will have insight into because she respects you as someone who has the pulse of the market. This chapter reveals how to develop this type of rapport in ways that come across as authentic and genuine because it shines through that you have the executive's best interests at heart.

We asked salespeople who cover a portfolio of small and medium-size enterprises how they reach executives in those companies. By eliminating times known to be set aside for internal meetings and learning something about the executive's personal schedule, some salespeople are able to divine answers as precise as, "Tuesday mornings from 7:30 to 8:15 a.m., or every second Friday at 4:00 p.m. at the golf course." They have it down to a tee! These salespeople also confirm that in medium-sized companies, it is often the owner-operator executive who turns off the lights at night—so a call that is placed after working hours is likely to be answered by the executive directly, or by a front desk security guard who will typically transfer your call right through.

We asked salespeople who cover a portfolio of large enterprises how they reach executives in those companies. A typical description of that environment is:

> You need a road map to navigate the maze of presidents, senior vice presidents, vice presidents, junior executives, directors, consultants, and various other chiefs. And even when you've figured

out whose department a project resides in, there's no guarantee that you can find who owns the pain. Plus you must contend with an army of personal assistants whose job it is to protect their boss's calendar from anyone who's not already on the approved list.

However, most of these salespeople agreed that an executive's assistant hears his boss on the phone all day, attends many of the same meetings, and understands what's topical and what a valuable idea looks like. Therefore, courting the assistant as though he were the executive himself shows respect for the role he plays and often opens doors that might otherwise remain closed.

And there are always examples of personal ingenuity. Here are two:

- *A computer hardware salesperson* whose territory spanned the area from Seattle to Salt Lake City to San Diego recalls that at one company, while he waited in the lobby for his appointments, he watched how people leaving the building treated the receptionist with respect as they walked out the door. The receptionist at this company was a mature lady who was always immaculately dressed and coiffured, and everybody, regardless of rank, made a point of nodding or talking with Barbara.

  One day this salesperson asked a mentor about the unusual deference people were paying, and he learned that Barbara was the company's fourth-largest shareholder and one of its original founders. She had traded a corner office for the front desk, where she could be the first face that greeted customers and could hear all the unguarded conversations that vendors and partners had in the lobby. Barbara served as a sentinel to protect her company's interests, and she had a direct line to all her executive peers. Needless to say, the salesperson in question cultivated a cordial relationship with Barbara, and shared his ideas on initiatives that he felt her company would benefit from. Accordingly, his ability to meet that company's executives increased.

- *A supplier of software* to a telecommunications company was so frustrated by what she described as "the high level of dysfunction, politics, and ass covering" in her client's business that she wrote a 30-page report titled "20 Reasons Why Selling to You Sucks." Maybe she'd watched Tom Cruise deliver his mission statement in *Jerry Maguire* one too many times. But she cared about her client as much as she cared about her quota, and she could not restrain herself. She printed only one copy, bound it in a faux leather cover, and hand-delivered it in a large envelope.

  The next two weeks felt like an eternity. Every morning she expected her sales director to call her in to account for her impulsiveness. She began to wonder if she'd done the right thing. Sixteen days later, she received a phone call inviting her to lunch with the customer CEO. After exchanging pleasantries, he asked her two questions: "Are you confident that what you wrote is accurate?" to which she told him she was. Then he asked, "Why are you telling me things that even my own staff members don't admit to?" to which she replied that while she did not know the answer, she was sure that this lack of communication was getting in the way of the company's moving forward. The CEO agreed, and within two months he had seconded this outspoken salesperson to his company for six months, granting her a roving commission and wide powers to root out the problems and initiate change.

  In return, the salesperson's company would be given any contract it wanted to bid on during that six-month period, and her company made hundreds of thousands of dollars from the arrangement. Unsurprisingly, the salesperson accepted a full-time role in her client's company after the six months were over so that she could finish what she'd started, but her successor in the sales role continued to enjoy several years of prosperity because his predecessor had had the courage to give an executive something to really think about. Executives love to be challenged and solve problems when salespeople serve as peers instead of hucksters.

In asking salespeople who call on small, medium, and large companies how they reach executives, we found that, while tales like the ones just given provide some anecdotal value, they are not as valuable as hearing from C-level executives themselves.

The executives we talked to in our research projects complained about receiving too many calls from "people who think I ought to be involved in every purchase. It's a real aggravation because they are selling above where they need to be, and they clearly don't understand or care about how our process operates." Calling on the wrong executive not only wastes the time and resources of salespeople, but also damages their credibility and their chances of a future relationship with that executive.

IDENTIFYING THE RELEVANT EXECUTIVE

Competitive salespeople don't waste people's time, least of all their own. They identify the *relevant executive* for each sales opportunity, and they take time to understand the dynamics of their customer's organization to uncover where influence, power, and control over a particular project reside. "It doesn't have to be the CEO of a corporation," said one respondent. "It could be someone who has great influence with very little formal rank." We are reminded of Barbara the receptionist.

To determine the right person to target, executives suggest that salespeople ask two questions.

"Who Will Really Evaluate, Decide, or Approve the Decision?"

An executive who initiates a project often reserves the decision-maker or approver role before she hands down the role of evaluating vendors to others. By way of definition, a *decision maker* is the person who analyzes the results of a formal team of evaluators, listens to recommendations, and then makes the final commitment to a vendor or to a certain course of action. There is usually one decision maker who makes that commitment.

On the other hand, an *approver* is usually a more senior person who reserves the right to review and approve or veto the decisions made by the decision maker. If the decision maker owns the budget and is trusted to make choices that are in the company's interests, the approver serves to offer objectivity but typically rubber-stamps what the decision maker wants to do. If the decision maker is new, under scrutiny, or about to leave the company, the approver's role becomes more active to safeguard the right decision.

As a rule, the executive who holds the highest rank and greatest influence regarding a particular project is the person you should always be sure to spend time with. This is the *relevant executive* associated with the sales opportunity. Another way to determine the relevant executive is to find the highest ranking executive who stands to gain the most or lose the most as a result of the project or application associated with the sales opportunity. Anyone above this person who is not involved in the project or is not affected by it is not an appropriate contact. Anyone below this person does not have a broad enough view of the project, can give you bad or misleading information, and through ignorance of the issues can even extend the sales cycle unnecessarily.

"Who Has the Highest Rank and Greatest Influence?"

Every company has the formal structure of leaders and followers, ranks and reporting lines. You see the structure and ranks printed in annual reports and on people's business cards. It's the legitimate chain of command that companies need in order to preserve order and divide labor, and it is easy to identify. Some people obsess about climbing that hierarchy as a means of securing wealth, power, and control. But if rank works as a constant, do eight vice presidents in the same company all exert identical levels of influence? Rarely. Influence is the informal, political power that people wield. It rarely maps along the lines of a formal hierarchy, which makes it difficult to see. In reality, it operates exactly like a personal currency in that it rises and falls with how much of it is *created, stored, borrowed, consolidated, exchanged,* or *spent.* It is also affected by the relative influence of others in the community.

THE DYNAMICS OF ORGANIZATIONAL INFLUENCE

People *gain influence* and control from their level of involvement in and value to a discussion or project (*created*), by past contributions that still confer a level of credibility and respect (*stored*), by powerful people or brands they are associated with or anointed by (*borrowed*), and by how popular a person or idea becomes, and the level of support and number of people who back it (*consolidated*).

People *lose influence* and control when the people or more influential brands that they were associated with go away or fall from grace, whereupon the influence that was borrowed or consolidated reverts to the amount of influence a person holds on his own (*exchanged*). People also lose influence by making mistakes, making enemies, or simply becoming has-beens whose stored supply of influence is depleted (*spent*).

As Janet Jackson crooned on her third album (coincidentally titled *Control*), we should all ask ourselves, "What have you done for me lately?" and take stock of our personal currency with the various stakeholders we want to be involved with, inside and outside the business arena. This is because influence doesn't have much of a shelf life. It doesn't store well.

So how do you identify a relevant executive who (1) is involved in a buying decision, (2) has a personal interest in the outcome, (3) has

adequate rank to affect the formal decision process, and (4) has suffi-
cient influence to affect the informal decision process? Executives we
interviewed told us that there are four things to look for:

- *What people have done* (their track record)
- *What people do now* (their value)
- *Whom people know* (their network)
- Their *ability to drive change* (their will)

Their Track Record

Psychologists will tell you that the most reliable indication of future
performance is past performance. People who have influence have a
track record of consistent success. This doesn't mean that they are
always successful. It means that they are *consistently* successful. When
you hear that someone is "on a roll" or enjoying "a lucky streak," or
when her "stars are in alignment," watch closely and you'll see that
"success begets success." Success has a muscle memory, so when
people enjoy success in one area of their life, they leverage their value
and their network of associates to exert their will on their surround-
ings across several fields. That's influence. When you are trying to
identify the relevant executive, look for patterns of success or lack of
success in an individual's personal or work history. People with no
track record have no currency to invest in the influence game.

Their Value

People build their track record in a number of different ways, but the
key to maintaining it over time is creating value for their company, its
executives, their customers, their peers, their partners, and other
stakeholders. That's what you get recognized for; that's where you
gain a reputation. The value may be personal and qualitative, such as
introducing someone to a new idea or a topical book or news article,

introducing him to people in your network who can help him, or simply bringing him useful information. Or the value may be commercial and quantitative. But as stated earlier, the influence you gain from these moments of glory soon fades once time outweighs the impact of your past contribution.

Value is, therefore, an everyday pursuit. You need to keep the iron hot. When you are trying to identify the relevant executive, look for the people who understand and can articulate what value looks like to their company, who are also contributing to delivering that value—as validated by their name being linked to all the right projects and talked about in all the right circles. Look for the people who are regarded as movers and shakers. If they are perceived as creating value, have a decent track record, and are connected to the sale you hope to make, they're candidates for being the relevant executive.

Their Network

The next marker we look for is each person's network: her tribe, grapevine, posse, alma mater, or power base. People who build influence are always plugged in to an informal chain of command, serving as either the hub or one of the spokes. They recognize their own limitations and surround themselves with people who can compensate for those limitations and balance them out. For example, new staff members who understand how influence works will connect with the alpha dog to learn the ropes and gain protection or favor. Old-timers will always nurture their allies inside and outside of their organization to stay current. Just as in the adage "birds of a feather flock together," sometimes these networks are made up of people who went to college or an MBA course together, past colleagues in another company, or people who worked together on various projects in the same company. People tap into these networks for information, for advice, and for favors. All members of a network are bound by mutual advantage, what the Chinese call the rule of *guanxi*.

Easily understood as "I'll scratch your back, then you scratch mine," *guanxi* (pronounced *guan-shee*) is a fundamental tenet in Asian cultures whereby people become trusted as "insiders" through the mutual exchange of information, favors, or other forms of value. According to Luo Yadong's book *Guanxi and Business* (World Scientific Publishing Company, 2007), the Mandarin word *guan* originally meant "a door"; its extended meaning *xi* is "to close up," meaning that behind the embrace of the closed door, you may be "one of us," but outside the door, your existence is barely recognized.

People who are "inside the door" of a network know about events before they happen; they're connected. In Italy there is a phrase for this: *radio scarpa*. The literal translation means "shoe radio," and the colloquial etymology refers to people who know what's going on simply by walking around, as though their very shoes could decode signals from every office in the company via the floorboards. Understanding this, a shrewd salesperson will know that if she doesn't know who the relevant executive is, or cannot reach him, the best approach is to broadcast her value to people on the grapevine. Sooner or later her message will reach the relevant executive.

To identify these players, always look for the people whose names are linked to many projects and discussions; look for the people who attend meetings and say very little, but whose few questions demonstrate deep insight that's beyond what they've heard from you; look for the people whose opinions others defer to, regardless of their rank; look for the people who seldom act surprised when they hear breaking news.

Without support from an executive's allies, it can be difficult to gain access.

Their Will

People with influence exert their will on the company; they set things in motion and change the status quo, and people follow them. But they seldom do it from their first day on the job. When a person joins a business, he learns how things work within the culture—how decisions are made, how ideas are discussed, even how people generally dress and speak. The way it works in business is the same way it works in college: you assimilate and work within a culture, or you get branded as an outsider. People build influence by first acclimating to the pervading belief system of how things should work (the company's *philosophy*) and working within the rules (the company's *policies*).

A former executive of Telecom New Zealand who was given the task of driving business transformation in a company that was resistant to change recalls:

> You can't afford to scare the horses, or they'll bolt and you'll never catch them. Even though you're the only white horse in the herd, you must throw on a blanket that makes you look like a brown horse, and get close to all the other brown horses so that they get to know you. Over time, you can let the blanket drop until they see that you're a white horse. But by then you've eaten the same hay and galloped in the same fields long enough that the horses have learned to trust you as one of their own. And of course, when the right horses neigh in your favor, the rest of the herd follows.

He first operated within the philosophy and policies of his company, created value, built a track record, and developed his network with various stakeholders so that he could drive change that would be supported.

This is how people with influence exert their will. When they have enough support from the right people, they can begin to interpret company policies as soft guidelines instead of hard rules, and find ways to change those policies for the benefit of the business. When a person reaches this level of influence, her personal philosophies start to be manifested in official ways, regardless of her official rank.

Donald T. Regan (1918–2003) was a tough-talking Wall Street financier who was appointed by U.S. president Ronald Reagan as his chief of staff, a role he was ousted from in February 1987. In his tell-all book *For the Record: From Wall Street to Washington* (Harcourt, 1988), Regan revealed that First Lady Nancy Reagan regularly consulted with astrologer Joan Quigley, whose exchanges shaped government policy as a result of Nancy's pillow talk with the president. Regan blamed his being fired on the first lady and her tarot card reader, neither of whom held any official rank, but who had plenty of influence. He writes: "Virtually every major move and decision the Reagans made during my time as White House chief of staff was cleared in advance with a woman in San Francisco who drew up horoscopes."

Dèng Xiǎopíng (1904–1997) never held office as head of state, but he served as de facto leader of the People's Republic of China from 1978 to the early 1990s. He was widely regarded as having backroom control without official rank. U.N. Secretary-General Kofi Annan said that Deng was the "primary architect of China's modernization and dramatic economic development,"[1] which included the revitalization of Shanghai's Pudong New Area as China's new economic hub, and the foundations for China's eventual entry into the World Trade Organization, which significantly changed the global economy.

Karl Rove (1950–) ran a company that managed direct mail, telephone polling, and fund-raising; according to the *Atlantic Monthly* magazine,[2] he was the primary strategist for 41 statewide, congressional, and national races between 1981 and 1999, of which his candidates won 34. That's a lot of friends in high places. He was appointed by George H. W. Bush to advise on the 1980 presidential campaign, in which Rove was fired mid-campaign for leaking information. Such was Rove's influence that he was rehired to handle direct mail for the 1984 Reagan-Bush and 1992 Bush presidential campaigns, from which he was fired again for leaking information. He returned to advise George W. Bush in his campaign to become governor of Texas in 1994, in his 1998 reelection campaign, and in his 2000 and 2004 presidential campaigns. Following the 2004 U.S. presidential election, Bush referred to Rove as "the architect" because of his role in taking Bush to the White House. Rove later became regarded as "Bush's brain" and the real power behind the throne.[3] It is unlikely that Rove could have exerted his will without his track record, his value, and his network, all of which he had carefully assembled throughout his career.

People without influence lack the power to work outside the boundaries set by others and must view policies as rules that cannot be broken. People with influence can interpret and modify an organization's rules as though they were mere guidelines. While others might be punished for doing so, those who are influential routinely have their acts legitimized as correct under the circumstances of the moment.

So to learn which people have influence, we must profile the stakeholders in a customer's business, looking at all these factors. When we do this, front-runners quickly and clearly come into focus. But beware: multiple people can all have various levels of influence. The final question we must address is: "Which person is most influential with regard to this sale?"

To find the answer to this, we explored whether there are degrees of influence and how to tell the difference. Company executives and successful account managers confirmed that influence is like energy— most of the time the influence of the people you're selling to lies dormant as stored or potential energy. It's not until something happens that the potential energy is released as kinetic energy and is set in motion to act upon the environment. It's in times of change that a person's influence is most apparent.

For example, when a new policy says that managers must obey a hiring freeze, but one department continues to hire without adverse consequences, this may indicate that the manager has enough influence to treat the rules that others must abide by as mere guidelines. When your customer undergoes a restructuring, a merger, or an acquisition, watch closely who consolidates his power or has new roles created for him, compared to those who see their empires unravel. Often those changes appear as a flash of lightning in the night sky, when everything is suddenly illuminated. Changes like that don't happen overnight or without prior discussion; people either *decide* what should happen, *make* those things happen, or *wonder* what happened.

Those who decide what happens are usually the most influential. These people control outcomes and shape what happens by defining the organization's goals and objectives. They surround themselves with trusted lieutenants who serve as their eyes, ears, and arms to make things happen. Because of their connections, they understand what is going on before it occurs, can anticipate what changes are taking place, and avoid the traps and dead ends that others blunder into.

Because influence doesn't follow the hierarchical lines of authority, it is possible for a junior staff member who has huge subject matter expertise to be at the hub of a decision-making process, enlisting a higher-ranked boss to legitimize her ideas by creating or rewriting a formal project. This is an example of influence flowing up from subordinate to superior. It can also flow sideways from peer to peer, and, as established earlier, external parties holding no rank at all can exert influence on a group. Influence can also flow from the boss down to the members of his staff, although when this happens it is more difficult to know whether you're watching the effect of influence or simply rank at work.

We might picture this informal structure as three concentric circles, as seen in Figure 4.1.

The inner circle (those who decide what happens) holds the highest influence and is surrounded by its network of allies and trusted resources (who make things happen for those in the inner circle). On the periphery is everyone else who gets involved in a project solely because formal roles require it. These people typically wield power only in proportion to their titles.

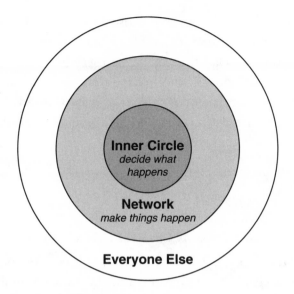

Figure 4.1 Degrees of Influence

The closer to the center someone is located, the more influence that person holds. It's here that the relevant executive for any sales opportunity will be found, for the inner circle is composed of those people who typically find ways to initiate projects that require funding and who have the most to gain or lose based on the outcomes. Like the modern-day parable that in a plate of bacon and eggs, the chicken is only a participant, whereas the pig is fully committed, so it is with those relevant executives in the inner circle who have skin in the game.

Because influence is situational, the people you find in the inner circle and their network will change from opportunity to opportunity. It's important for you to understand this, because some salespeople we have consulted fall into the trap of mapping the politics and influence in their key accounts for one deal and then expecting those things to remain constant in the next deal. Influence is always in motion as a by-product of the nature of each opportunity and who needs to be involved in the buying process, the incumbency of current suppliers, who wants to preserve those suppliers and who wants to replace them, whether a project fits within a department's discretionary spending levels or needs to be escalated, and the fact that people fall into and out of favor all the time. People may leave, and new people with allegiances of their own may be hired. There are so many variables that we recommend that you profile influence one opportunity at a time.

Once you've identified the right executive to sell to, the next question is how to gain access.

GAINING ACCESS TO EXECUTIVES

According to our research with C-level executives, the most effective way to gain access is through a recommendation by someone in the executive's company (see Figure 4.2). A full 84 percent of executives said that they would *usually* or *always* grant a meeting with a salesperson who was recommended internally. This highlights the importance of building companywide relationships that open doors to senior management.

	Always	Usually	Occasionally	Never
Recommendation from someone in your company	16%	68%	16%	0%
Referral from someone outside your company	8%	36%	44%	12%
A letter or e-mail, followed by a telephone call	4%	20%	40%	36%
Cold call by telephone	0%	20%	36%	44%
Contact at an off-site event	0%	44%	32%	24%

Figure 4.2 Scorecard of Methods for Gaining Access to Executives

84

Other methods did not fare as well. Referrals from outside the organization are sometimes successful, yet more than half of executives will never or only occasionally meet with a salesperson who has been recommended by an outside contact. Cold calling ranked the lowest, with only 20 percent of participants saying that they would *usually* grant a meeting as a result, while 44 percent said that they would *never* respond to cold calls. A letter or e-mail sent before the call improves the odds only slightly.

With 84 percent of executives saying that they would *usually* or *always* meet a salesperson if that salesperson were recommended internally (87 percent in China), the study clearly indicates that establishing relationships at lower levels of the organization is critical before trying to access the executive's calendar. One CEO explained that he would grant a meeting "when I see or hear something that might be applicable in my world, or at the request of some of my cohorts around here."

These "cohorts" are part of the executive's influence network; they may be a friend of someone in the executive's inner circle, an internal consultant, or a low-level employee within the organization who just happens to have credibility with an inner-circle executive.

Competitive salespeople understand and work the influence networks within their customer's organization. "I'm always trying to find someone I can approach to mentor me and help maneuver my message through the account," said one sales executive. "I strive to build a win/win relationship by finding people who can benefit from this relationship. They actually sponsor your effort to reach senior executives."

Our China research provided scores with similar highs and lows, with a variance of plus or minus 3 percent. But in talking with directors of government-run enterprises, managers of private companies, and the executives of foreign-owned companies trading in China, we found some new reasons *why* Chinese executives prefer to meet salespeople only after they receive a recommendation from someone they trust.

To explain it, we're going to need a quick history lesson to help you understand where they're coming from.

Understanding the Mindset of Chinese Executives

Six hundred years ago, China was a political, an intellectual, a military, and an economic colossus. In his groundbreaking work *1421: The Year China Discovered America* (Harper, 2004), Gavin Menzies contrasts China's position on the fifteenth-century world stage with that of the major European powers of the time, and concludes that in every way, China ruled supreme:

> At the inauguration of emperor Zhu Di's Forbidden City in Beijing on 2 February 1421, 26,000 dignitaries ate a ten-course banquet served on fabulous porcelain. At the feast to celebrate the coronation of Catherine of Valois as Queen of England on 21 February 1421, 600 guests ate one course of salted cod on slabs of stale bread that served as plates. Zhu Di's walled city was more than 1400 times the size of the walled City of London. Later that year, King Henry VI went to war against France commanding an army of 5000 men who he ferried across the English Channel in four fishing boats. In the same year, Emperor Zhu had a standing army of one million men.
>
> The Emperor had more than 1350 warships, 3000 merchant vessels and 400 grain transports, plus an armada of 250 treasure ships equipped with cannons and rockets that transported 30,000 men around the world. Each ship was 400 feet long. By contrast, Columbus' Santa Maria was 82 feet long, about the size of one of Zhu's ship rudders.
>
> The Silk Road was open all the way to Persia. China's industrial system was flourishing. Forward bases had been opened around the Indian Ocean. The way was clear for Zhu Di's greatest gamble yet—the entire world was to be brought into Confucian harmony.

Yet within 150 years, a change in policy saw China reverse its expansionist policies, scrap its navies, and burn its shipyards. It entered a long sleep, where it remained while other world powers emerged during the Industrial Revolution. In the 300 years that followed, China was embroiled in various wars and rebellions, mounting debts, the loss of Hong Kong to British rule, and the eventual end to 5,000 years of imperial rule. China first became a republic in 1912; this republic was overturned by a prime minister who declared himself the new emperor in 1915, then "died" a year later, leaving a power vacuum that was greedily filled by ruthless warlords who carved the country into fiefdoms.

After World War I, the revolutionary Sun Yat-Sen set out to unite his fragmented nation through an alliance with the Communist Party of China and with help from the Soviets. His protégé, Chiang Kai-shek, disagreed with communist rule and seized control of the rival Nationalist Party, using military force to defeat the southern and central warlords. He then waged war on the Communist Party itself in 1927 and drove its supporters to the northwest in what became known as the Long March, during which the communists reorganized under Chairman Mao Zedong. China then endured 14 years of tumult that included the Japanese invasion and World War II, during which time the communists succeeded in winning popular support. Facing oblivion, Chiang Kai-shek fled with his Nationalist Party to form the government of Taiwan in 1949, the same year that the People's Republic of China was formed as a new nation on the mainland. Today's tension between China and Taiwan originated here.

Chairman Mao instituted the Great Leap Forward, an attempt to lift the economy by mandating the production of steel in backyard furnaces, which Mao promised would turn China into a world-class steel producer to rival the United States and the United Kingdom. This was a massive financial and humanitarian disaster that saw the country denuded of trees and labor diverted from harvesting to melt pots and pans. Worthless cheap iron, famine, starvation, and around

40 million deaths were the result of this pipe dream. Mao stepped down in 1959 and was replaced by new leaders.

And China heard: "Don't believe promises, only facts."

In 1978 China became a market economy, and in 2001 it entered the World Trade Organization and opened its borders to foreign business. As the world shifted production to low-cost Chinese mills and factories, China became cash rich. In a bid to acquire the legitimacy of western marques, it has attempted or completed partial or whole acquisitions of the following:

- IBM's PC division
- General Electric's home appliance division
- Morgan Stanley
- Standard Bank (South Africa)
- PetroKazakhstan
- Fortis insurance
- Rio Tinto
- MG Rover automotive
- Unocal oil
- Maytag appliances
- Marconi telecommunications

Decades after Mao's communal privations, China's nouveaux riche have responded to Deng's battle cry, "To get rich is glorious," going from nothing to everything in just a few years. In preparation for the 2008 Beijing Olympics and 2010 Shanghai World Expo, massive capital expenditures were made to modernize those cities. According to some sources, almost a quarter of the world's 150,000 construction cranes are now in China. As *Time* magazine journalist Hannah Beech writes:

To be suddenly wealthy in China is to be engaged in a full-blown, keeping-up-with-the-Chans spending contest. In June, a

Bentley sold for 8.8 million yuan ($1.06 million) at a Beijing auction—apparently because eight is a lucky number, not because the car was worth that amount. In the gambling paradise of Las Vegas, Chinese jet-setters have displaced Japanese industrialists as the most prevalent—and most welcome—group of high rollers. Chinese entrepreneurs don't tend to do the Jeff Bezos thing—dressing down in wrinkled khakis. *"In China, if you're rich, you have to look the part,"* says Wang Deyuan, who owns one of the top ad agencies in southern China. *"You have to show you have money, otherwise no one believes that you're rich."*[4]

And China heard: "If you can't see it, it isn't real."

"I'll believe it when I see it" is a common sentiment. This is a product of the executive wanting to remain at a safe distance in case things go pear-shaped; he can't lose face if the salesperson is managed through an intermediary. But once value is exchanged and future value is offered, a Chinese executive will be more willing to allow the relationship to be transferred. When this occurs, the person who referred the salesperson gains face under the rules of *guanxi*.

So the rule of thumb when trying to gain access to a Chinese executive is to be patient and work through trusted intermediaries until the executive is ready to deal directly. It can take a year—some say two—for the executive to see that you're in for the long haul. Your company brand can help you open doors, but ultimately it's the longevity of a personal relationship that executives are after, along with access to your personal network—again, *guanxi* at work.

If two vendors have a similar product, but one has a prestigious brand, association with the prestigious brand will win every time. If two vendors have similar products and equally prestigious brands, but one salesperson is known around town and has a strong network of associates, it's the relationship exchange that will win every time.

Think of it as one giant game of Facebook and LinkedIn, where your reputation and the people you know are as good as hard currency.

HOW DO EXECUTIVES SCREEN AND TEST SALESPEOPLE?

The first gauntlet you run when you're trying to meet any executive is the system of roadblocks that are put in place to preserve her calendar or diary. You must find a path through these screens and filters, and then introduce yourself in a way that will cause the executive to give you a meeting.

Roadblocks don't exist just to make life difficult for salespeople. Most of the time they're a legitimate mechanism that has been put in place to help the executive focus on important tasks rather than distractions.

Why Do Roadblocks Exist?

In some companies, getting calendar time with a senior executive may happen only if you contact the executive assistant or the executive's secretary. You simply can't get on the executive's calendar by contacting him directly. In that case, you may have to either use a sponsor or treat the assistant as a resource to help you schedule a meeting with the executive.

The chief causes of roadblocks are the following:

1. Executives delegate meetings of this type.
2. It's the formal process used in this organization.
3. The executive is too busy to schedule meetings with external suppliers.
4. The executive's previous experience with salespeople suggests that they should be seen by lower-level executives first.

Figure 4.3 Causes of Roadblocks

Getting Past the Roadblocks

We've provided a worksheet in Appendix 2 for planning how to bypass the roadblocks you face. The techniques that can be used to address them include the following:

- When there's an organizational change in your company, suggest having a meeting to explain the new structure.
- Suggest a meeting with an equivalent-level executive from your organization (like-rank selling).
- Accept redirections to meet other executives or people of lower rank, but always ask the executive to make an introduction and request a follow-up meeting to review the outcomes.
- Schedule a meeting with an executive to communicate past value delivered or to confirm your ongoing value.
- Contact the executive when there's any significant event in the customer's market, even if it's unrelated to the current sales campaign. Executives like to know that you're thinking about them, even if there's nothing for you to sell.

The stakes are high if you cannot access the relevant executive. Some of the latest data from companies whose sales cycles are nine months or more indicate that it may cost more than $200,000 to pursue an opportunity, whether you win or not. That's a significant sum to bet on selling to low-level managers. If you don't have the chance to get past the gatekeepers and meet the relevant executive, it may be prudent to walk away and save the cost of sale.

There's one other word of caution that bears mentioning at this point: don't attempt to circumvent the gatekeeper unless you have a high degree of confidence that you can obtain the meeting with the executive. As one savvy salesperson put it: "Hell hath no fury like a gatekeeper scorned!" Once she is around a roadblock, a salesperson will be quickly tested. CXOs told us that salespeople who get past their roadblocks on a cold call get five minutes to show that they can add value. Here are some tips:

- Speak from a business perspective and don't get caught up in the "bells and whistles" of product features.
- Raise relevant questions and share business perspectives that are new to the executive.
- If you're an incumbent, point out the potential limitations of your products in light of changing demands and provide ideas for making improvements, thus enhancing your credibility.

CHOOSING A PATH

After you've evaluated whether it's more advisable to work with the gatekeepers or to go around them, you'll need to decide how to navigate that path to the executive. How do you go from where you are today to gaining an audience? Most salespeople know at least four approaches for achieving access to senior executives (see Figure 4.4). As Figure 4.2 showed earlier, some of these approaches are more successful than others.

Overt	Sponsor	Referral	Gatekeeper
Implement an overt approach via the telephone or by making a phone call preceded by a letter or an e-mail	Use a credible sponsor within the client's organization to help secure access	Use a referral (someone outside the client's organization), such as a consultant, business associate, or friend	Treat the gatekeeper (AA, secretary, or the like) as a resource and use that person to help secure access

Figure 4.4 Tactics to Gain Access to Executives

Overt

An overt approach is one in which you contact the executive directly. This type of approach can be accomplished by a direct telephone call, or by a telephone call preceded by a letter or an e-mail. However, don't be surprised if the overt approach leads to your being sent down to lower levels. Our research revealed that 44 percent of executives would *never* respond to this approach, and only 36 percent said that they would respond *occasionally.*

Sponsor

With this approach, someone inside the client's organization helps you gain access. It's absolutely critical that the sponsor have credibility with the executive. In our research, executives said that this was the most effective way to secure access to them. In fact, 68 percent said that they *usually* grant an audience to salespeople sponsored by a credible person within their own organization, and 16 percent said that they *always* do so.

Referral

With a referral approach, someone outside the client's organization (such as a business associate, consultant, or friend of the executive) helps you secure access to the executive. In most cases, this is an effective way to reach the executive. As with a sponsor, the referral's credibility with the executive is critical to success.

Gatekeeper

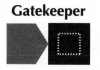

Try treating gatekeepers as though they were the executive. Explain your proposition and ask their opinions. The best executive assistants will be conversant with their boss's key business issues and will immediately see your value. The poor ones won't understand the discussion but may pass you forward because you *sound* like you belong. If you are successful in obtaining a gatekeeper's support, keep him in the loop.

INITIAL CONTACT WITH THE EXECUTIVE

In Appendix 2, there is a template for an initial telephone call to the executive. You can use this template to help you prepare to contact the executive for the first time. It contains five simple steps:

1. Preparing Your Approach

Simply put, you want the executive to perceive you as being prepared, succinct, and confident. This call should not last more than three or four minutes. If you can determine an executive's personal agenda and address it while also addressing her business agenda, you will have easily developed competitive differentiation.

2. Introduction

Begin with a brief introduction that clearly states who you are and why you're contacting the executive. Explain your connection to your sponsor or referrer, if appropriate. You have only one opportunity to make a first good impression! This is particularly important if this is your first meeting with the executive. You want to make certain the executive understands that you did some level of preparation prior to the meeting.

3. Purpose

Explain the purpose of the call. You'll have to explain to the executive why you're calling him. This could be to arrange a meeting to discuss a specific business issue that you understand to be compelling to the executive. Paraphrasing what hundreds of senior executives told us consistently: "One of the single best ways for a salesperson to gain credibility at my level is to listen before proposing a solution. This is the number one trait I look for in salespeople I would consider as candidates to be one of my Trusted Advisors."

4. Credibility

Explain the homework you've done on the executive's organization, or perhaps cite the past value you've delivered to the organization if this call is to an executive in an existing client organization. Another option is to describe how you've helped other companies address similar challenges.

5. Commitment to Action

Propose a clear and specific action or next step, such as a meeting. Executives like to be told what you expect them to do. Have a set of next steps ready to request at the meeting with the executive, and be willing to be held accountable for accomplishing them.

If the executive refers you to someone at a lower level in the organization, this may not be the result you wanted, but it isn't a train wreck either. The executive may simply be referring you to someone in her network of advisors who is better suited to evaluate the discussion. It always helps to do three things:

1. Ask the executive for an introduction to the person, because this is far better than your having to call him cold. You can leverage the fact that his boss sent you to talk.
2. Ask her what she hopes you will achieve with her subordinate, and what additional people are suited to have the discussion with you. Turn it into a networking opportunity.
3. Ask to reconnect with the executive to review how what you hear from her subordinates compares to the level of readiness in other companies for which you've solved the same problem. Executives typically like to know how their company benchmarks, so use the occasion to demonstrate your value as someone with insight beyond the executive's silo walls.

Here's what one sales professional shared about this topic:

My customer went through a management reorganization, which eroded some of my support base. I had a good relationship with the engineering manager who was promoted to COO when the former COO was promoted to CEO. I wanted to get close to the new CEO, so I called my contact for advice. The COO confirmed my ideas about the issues that were of most importance to the CEO, and agreed to support my solution if I was successful in getting it positioned.

I then contacted the CEO and asked to meet with him. After explaining the ways I felt we could add value, he said it didn't make sense for us to meet unless I first had the support of a mid-level manager whom I'd never met and didn't know existed. I could have perceived this to be a negative outcome. But it was clear that this person's opinion mattered to the CEO: she was in his personal network. I did a thorough discovery of the firm's key business drivers, and after the meeting she sent an e-mail to the CEO suggesting that it was a good idea to discuss future opportunities in more detail.

This is a clear example of how being referred down can grant you credibility with other key players, and in return enhance your credibility with the executive who sent you there in the first place.

With these tips, you're on your way to securing a first meeting with the executive even when you're making a cold call, albeit a well-researched one! However, if your company provides air support in the form of marketing campaigns designed to trouble the executive about business problems he faces that your company can solve, your chances of success are greatly magnified because the executive is already warmed up to recognize that he has the problem, and he already knows that your company plays in the space.

Whatever the approach, you're now ready to meet face to face, where the first item on your agenda is to establish your credentials and your credibility.

Chapter Summary

Let's summarize what we've discussed in this chapter about the second question in our research: "How do salespeople gain access to executives?" Let's break it down to the top three messages:

1. *Identify the relevant executive.*

   There is one person who most feels the pain and has skin in the game. If a project to find a supplier is already underway, the relevant executive is the person who first identified the need and had the credibility to turn it into a formal project backed by resources. If you're trying to create a project by tapping into a problem that the customer needs to solve, the relevant executive will be the person who has the most to gain or the most to lose. Many stakeholders will need to be met and developed as supporters. But at the center of the web is the executive who is most relevant to this decision. She may not always be at the very top of the company, so sell only as high as you need to. But a general rule of thumb is: *the bigger the pain, the higher the game.*

2. *Get close to the influencers.*

   Every decision to buy from a supplier involves several evaluators, one decision maker, and possibly several approvers. This is the formal decision process. Outside of that, there are other people who get involved who have influence disproportionate to their role. Some of these may not even be in the customer's organization. Finding the *power behind the throne* and aligning your sale with his agenda is critical. If you win the formal vendor evaluation but you don't have political support, you might lose the deal. If you lose the formal vendor evaluation but you have powerful influencers on your side, the formal criteria will change to justify your winning. Nobody says this is fair, but it's how every large investment decision is made, even in government contracts. Learn and master these rules; they're the only ones that really matter.

3. *Navigate the roadblocks.*

Executives test salespeople to see if they're worthy of an audience. Sometimes this is for sport, but most times it's to protect their calendar from time wasters. Their organization will include project leaders, executive assistants, and others who will tell you to deal solely with them, tell you to go away, or leave you hanging while you wait for them to return your call. There are several options you can choose for getting past the roadblocks, or even for converting the blockers into allies. When you choose to go around someone or over her head, you need to weigh the pros and cons of doing so based on the situation at hand. Research shows that using the telephone to cold-call an executive is the least effective method, with an 80 percent failure rate. Gaining a referral from someone the executive trusts is the most effective, with an 84 percent success rate. If you have strong marketing support that regularly troubles the executive about the problems he is facing, the referral to meet you will usually come from the executive himself.

Chapter 5

How to Establish Credibility at the Executive Level

Salespeople we've both worked with in our respective consulting practices speak of a moment of terror that occurs after they've stormed the gates, swung a grappling hook at the tallest tower, and climbed the rope to the top. As they finally stand in front of their target executive, how do they establish their credentials so that they can avoid being thrown back out the window? This chapter reveals what executives have told us you can do to win the keys to the kingdom.

Executives use their first personal meeting with a salesperson to answer specific questions:

- Does the salesperson understand our needs? Has he done his homework on our key business drivers?
- Has he been able to convey how his product or service applies to me? Why it is better than his competitors'?
- Is this individual an empowered decision maker, or will he have to consult his manager for decisions?
- Is the salesperson professional and confident, sharp (thinks on his feet and doesn't use canned speeches), honest (acknowledges potential shortcomings), and reflective (listens rather than tells)?

Just as salespeople are trying to qualify customers, so too are customers qualifying salespeople. Executives we have met with have revealed that they value dealing with salespeople who solved similar business problems for other customers. One executive said: "They understand that their solution may not be a panacea, and they deliver business value by helping me explore various options. My objective is to discuss and develop realistic solutions, not to see a slick sales presentation."

A CREDIBILITY GAP

While many of our interviews with executives focused on how salespeople need to engage more in terms of the Buyer's Journey and less in terms of an arbitrary sales cycle, selling is meaningless unless you can actually deliver the value you promise. We wondered how well most companies bring home the bacon after the sale is made. One executive summed up her experience with the following anecdote:

A man dies and finds himself at the Pearly Gates with both St. Peter and the devil. St. Peter says, "You're not supposed to die for another ten years. We'll have to send you back." The man is thrilled, but on his way out he sees one door to Heaven and another to Hell.

He hears a raging party behind the door to Hell and asks the devil standing guard if he can take a peek. The devil says, "Only for a minute." So he goes through the door to Hell and finds an incredible party, with endless food, champagne, music, and every rock star from history beckoning him to join them. He says, "If this is Hell, I want in!"

When he returns to Earth, he spends the next decade committing every sin he knows, and a few he had to look up on the Internet. Ten years to the day, he dies and meets the devil in front of the door to Hell. As the door opens, he hears no music and sees no party; only brimstone, fire, and the wailing of a thousand damned souls.

He cries, "Wait! Where's the party?" The devil smiles and explains, "Oh, ten years ago you were a prospect. Now you're a customer."

As you can see, this story exemplifies how salespeople promise a lot to get the sale—but often don't deliver on those promises.

Accordingly, our research asked: "What benefits did you expect versus what was delivered from strategic suppliers?" The criteria that executives commented on are not as instructive as the startling differences between expectation and delivery in each case.

As shown in Figure 5.1, most executives feel that they do not receive the expected benefits from strategic partners. Maybe the supplier failed

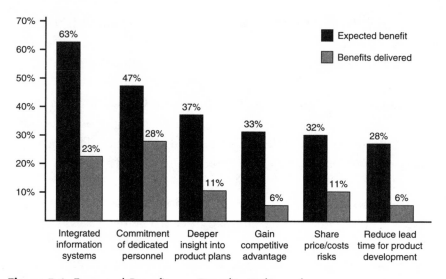

Figure 5.1 Expected Benefits vs. Benefits Delivered

in its delivery or the solution did not work as the executive hoped. Maybe the customer dropped the ball after taking delivery of the solution. Or perhaps the value was delivered and nobody closed the loop with the executive. Whatever the reasons, there is such a wide gap between the expected and realized benefits that it prompts the question, "What exactly do executives want from a sales organization?" One executive succinctly gave the answer as: "Integrity in the way a salesperson works with us, along with a track record of delivering on what was promised. Credibility is the product of those two."

All three studies reinforce this executive's interpretation (see Figure 5.2). According to the studies, building credibility comes from providing executives with a sense that you understand their business, you have the capability and experience to help them solve their problems, and your intention is to establish lasting relationships and become their Trusted Advisor. Credibility is the result of the value that a salesperson or a sales organization brings to the executive over the long term.

A demonstrated ability to think beyond the current sales opportunity is also critical to the executive's perception of a salesperson's credibility.

CRITERIA	STUDY 1 USA 1995 Av. Score (1–5)	STUDY 2 USA 1999 Av. Score (1–5)	STUDY 3 ASIA 2005 Av. Score (1–5)
Ability to marshal resources	4.44	4.18	4.23
Understood my business goals	4.40	4.52	4.65
Responsiveness to my requests	4.36	4.56	4.62
Willingness to be held accountable	4.32	4.70	4.81
Knowledge of company's products	4.08	4.11	4.14
Demonstrated ability to solve problems	4.00	4.31	4.24
Works well with my staff	3.96	3.79	3.81
Knowledge of my industry	3.88	3.70	3.75
Knowledge of their own industry	3.76	4.34	4.44
Track record of accomplishments	3.60	3.93	3.70
Understands my personal issues	3.32	3.03	3.21
Source of information about competitors	2.84	2.70	2.81
Length of service in job	2.48	2.40	1.81

Figure 5.2 Executives' Expectations of Salespeople

105

The sales organization must manage the relationship for the good of the customer, not simply from one sales opportunity to another.

Let's examine in some detail the top four criteria identified by executives as the key ingredients for building credibility with them (see Figure 5.2). What do they mean, and why are they important?

Ability to Marshal Resources

"Ability to marshal resources" was the single most important factor cited for building credibility in our original study. This represents a shift from the "lone wolf" salesperson toward building customer relationships involving multiple business functions. It also involves the formation of a virtual sales organization that is designed to bring the customer a total solution. Executives want comprehensive solutions that address their global business requirements. They also want a single point of contact within the sales organization who has responsibility and accountability for the solution.

This means that a single salesperson will not be able to go it alone. He may have to engage additional experts from within his own firm, coordinate across geographic boundaries, and work with a variety of business partners to help his customers solve complex business problems. Executives want to know that a salesperson can represent them within the salesperson's own organization and has the ability to get things done. According to one executive, "If salespeople bring the right resources to us, avoiding the 'sales mode' by staying in an 'action and results' mode, it builds a lot of confidence." The ability of salespeople to wield influence within their own organizations and to bring the right resources to bear on their customers' needs are of prime importance here.

Understands Business Goals and Objectives

A critical way in which salespeople can successfully establish credibility is by having the ability to understand the customers' needs, including their goals and their key business drivers. Business drivers can be defined as the internal and external pressures that create the need for change. These pressures can create both problems and opportunities for the customer, with specific consequences and paybacks. The most pressing problems and opportunities subsequently result in distinct business initiatives. Without that understanding, there is no reference point that the salesperson can use to gauge the fit of a product or service. Focusing solely on the sale—with no context of how a solution benefits the customer's world—will create the view that the salesperson "is interested only in the commission."

Responsive to Requests

Executives want to do business with people who respond to their needs. They want to know that "when the salesperson says she's going to do something, she will deliver." In most organizations, the ability to be responsive involves the salesperson's ability to bring the appropriate resources to bear on the customers' requirements. Therefore, to build credibility, not only does the salesperson need to be personally responsive, but she needs to have enough influence to convince others within her own organization to be responsive as well. One executive cited a salesperson's ability to "tell me what she can do and make certain she also tells me what she can't do—both are important." This same executive went on to say that it is also important to "make certain that you can deliver on what you say you can do."

Willingness to Be Held Accountable

Executives realize that problems will occur at some point in time—that's a fact of business life. But how those problems are handled is the difference between establishing credibility or culpability. Executives want to minimize conversations with different people who are unfamiliar with their situation. They want one point of contact within an organization for problem resolution.

One executive stated, "I want the salesperson to take ownership of the problem, recognize that it exists, and secure the resources to solve it. I don't want the problem to be mine. That's one of the reasons why I worked with someone outside our organization in the first place." Another executive took this point a step further by saying, "I look to people outside our organization to provide expertise that we don't have. We don't ask salespeople to do things we can do ourselves."

Knowing and understanding this, salespeople who provide business value to the customer will readily build credibility with customer executives.

Note that a salesperson's willingness to be held accountable rose to the number one rank in the second and third studies.

CLOSING THE CREDIBILITY GAP

Building credibility with senior-level customer executives is a critical factor in developing lasting business relationships. Becoming a Trusted Advisor to these executives should be a major objective of most salespeople involved in high-value, complex sales.

So how is credibility developed over the long term? It comes about when the salesperson demonstrates both his capability and his integrity. Figure 5.3 depicts the two components of credibility, with capability on the x axis and integrity on the y axis. If you've already met with the relevant executive, that person will have made some initial assumptions about the potential value you could bring to her organization, and perhaps even to her personally.

Salespeople who are seeking only a Problem Solver relationship will proceed only in the horizontal direction. It's clear that you must display your capability, but be careful that you don't become seen as merely an "extra pair of hands" or an "expert for hire," as this can lead

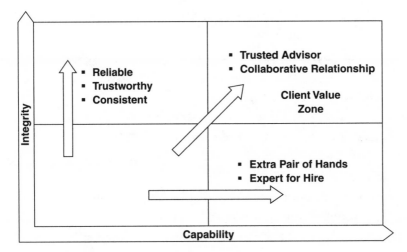

Figure 5.3 Components of Credibility

Source: Adapted from Jagdish Shoth and Andrew Sobel, *Clients for Life* (New York: Simon & Schuster, 2000).

to your being engaged only on a transactional basis, where your relationship will be managed at the lower levels.

To enhance the relationship, you must continually demonstrate your integrity and your customer focus, which will ultimately build trust. Your objective in moving in this direction is to be perceived as reliable on a consistent basis—someone whom the executive receives increasing exposure to by virtue of the value you start to add and get credit for. This is the hallmark of an Emerging Resource. But be careful that you don't build only the integrity of the relationship to the detriment of the capability aspect, or you might end up as the executive's best new friend who gets plenty of golfing dates but no sales!

To come to be perceived as a Trusted Advisor, you'll have to move up on both axes at the same time so that you can operate in the Client Value Zone. Here's where you'll come to be perceived as a Trusted Advisor and start to develop a collaborative relationship with the client executive. Trusted Advisors contribute to the client's success and view that success as critical to their own success.

You'll know you're in the Client Value Zone when the executive:

- Shares confidential information with you.
- Unveils his long-range plans to give you an advantage in preparing a response to his proposal.
- Asks you to come in at an early stage in his buying cycle to help establish the objectives of the project.
- Asks you for advice on issues that were unrelated to your company's solutions.
- Asks you to sit in on key strategic planning meetings or staff meetings, demonstrating that you are part of the client team.
- Values your success and demonstrates a keen interest in making you successful.
- Asks you to help him write a requirements definition for a new project—or even asks you to help him create an RFP, presentation, or other documents.
- Asks you to meet him at an off-site location so that he can reveal critical information to you.

"People buy from people they like" is an old sales adage. While this is a true saying, it's not entirely accurate when it comes to the way senior executives make buying decisions. Our research clearly indicates that personal feelings are usually not a factor. Instead, "people buy from people they trust" is a more accurate description.

"Say I've got a problem I need solved," says one executive. "I know two people who have expertise in that area. One of them I trust and respect. The other might actually have more expertise, but I don't know her as well. If I call the one I trust, I'll begin to act on his advice immediately. If I call the other one, I'll probably double-check and get a second opinion."

According to the executives, another essential factor in building trust is the salesperson's candor. Executives can sense when someone is not telling the whole story. Trust erodes quickly when an executive feels that the salesperson is not "coming clean." Executives stated that salespeople who misled them made them "wonder what other bombs may be waiting to explode." One executive realized that "there are challenges for all solutions to my business problems. I want to get as clear an indication as possible of what those are up front, warts and all."

Top-performing salespeople understand that building credibility at the executive level comes from providing the executive with a sense that they understand the business, they have the capability and experience to help the executive solve her business problems, and they intend to establish lasting relationships. This enables the salesperson to enhance the relationship and become the executive's Trusted Advisor. A salesperson's objective should be to move toward the upper right, in the direction of the Client Value Zone, as depicted in Figure 5.3.

Here's what one sales professional shared about this topic:

> My customer was number three in the check printing business, and volume had been increasing dramatically. Flush with funds, the CEO saw a window of opportunity to improve the company's manufacturing process and get ahead of its competitors. But most employees didn't see this vision and were content to increase capacity in an incremental fashion. Bidding for that work would have done little to help the customer, and would have been low value for us. I undertook an in-depth study of the company's manufacturing process and asked the CEO who was the best person to show me how it really worked. He introduced me to a manufacturing worker who was not a decision maker, but who was clearly trusted by the CEO. In fact he'd been challenged to develop new solutions in the manufacturing process. I agreed to spend time with him, with the proviso that I could return to the CEO to report our findings.
>
> The outcome of the study was a recommendation for a unique process-control computer that could manage the check printing

process to increase throughput by a factor of 20. The ROI was less than 12 months, and the solution would provide substantial growth over the next 10 years. During my presentation, the CEO kept nodding positively, then turned to his CFO and asked, "Do you see any reason why we shouldn't do this?" A year later the firm was number two in the market.

Remember, building credibility with executives by demonstrating both your technical or delivery capability and your personal integrity and customer focus is based almost entirely on your ability to interpret the executive's business drivers, as outlined earlier in the section in Chapter 3 titled "The Drivers of Executive Decision Making." You must frame your value in the context of your customers' world.

HOW TO MAKE AN IMPRESSION ON AN EXECUTIVE

It's obvious that salespeople cannot simply go in there and "wing it." Let's explore how you need to conduct yourself and what impression you need to leave (see Figure 5.4).

Demonstrated Accountability

Executives confirmed that they expect the buck to start and stop with you. They look for salespeople who are willing to be held accountable for both the success *and* the failure of their organization's ability to provide service and drive results. It turns an executive off when she hears a salesperson say that he cannot do something because he lacks the authority or control. When this happens, the sales rep is admitting to being roadkill, and the executive will see the vultures circling overhead and disengage from the Empty Suit Salesperson. Demonstrating accountability means taking the lumps when things go wrong (and having a plan to resolve the problems), being the single point of contact, and showing that a method for

CRITERIA	STUDY 1 USA 1995 Av. Score (1–5)	STUDY 2 USA 1999 Av. Score (1–5)	STUDY 3 ASIA 2005 Av. Score (1–5)
Demonstrated accountability	4.48	4.49	4.37
Understood my business goals	4.40	4.59	4.45
Listened before prescribing	4.36	4.59	4.71
Knowledge of industry/company	4.36	4.02	4.81
Had a game plan for next steps	4.20	3.79	4.14
Ability to solve problems	4.00	4.15	4.31
The meeting achieved stated objectives	4.00	3.79	3.52
Communicated value	3.96	3.95	4.59
Proposed alternative solutions	3.88	3.69	2.95
Thinking beyond the current sale	3.84	3.56	4.11
Works well with my staff	3.76	3.77	3.88
Prepared and followed a meeting agenda	3.48	3.52	4.20
Source of information about competitors	2.72	2.95	4.36

Figure 5.4 The First Meeting with a Senior Executive

measuring your contribution exists. Executives don't want you to represent your company to them as much as they want you to represent them to your company, and to be their agent on the inside who knows her way around the organization and can tap into the pockets of value to make a difference.

Those executives we tested in China told us that they don't look for accountability from an individual salesperson. Instead, they expect the salesperson to elevate them, brokering a relationship with a peer in the vendor organization so that they can speak with an equal. In a market in which annual attrition of salespeople can be as high as 75 percent, executives expect salespeople to open the door, but don't expect them to stick around long enough to be accountable for anything. This is another reason they crave peer relationships, as well as for *guanxi*. We expect that as Asian markets mature and people stay in roles longer, this criterion may adjust so that it is in line with what we see in other developed nations.

Understood My Business Goals

In the five years between the first and second research studies, a subtle shift occurred. Executives started rating "understood my business goals" and "listened before prescribing" higher than the previously more popular "demonstrated accountability." The change indicates that in a period of dot-com excess, budgets under scrutiny, and high stakes, executives wanted to know that the decisions they were making were backed by sound analysis and due diligence.

Together these top three criteria remain critical and were only made more relevant by the scandals involving Enron and Arthur Andersen, WorldCom, Barings Bank and Nick Leeson, Lloyds of London, Harshad Mehta of India, Parmalat of Italy, the Metallgesellschaft affair in Germany, Daiwa Bank and Toshihide Iguchi in Japan, the HIH Insurance collapse in Australia, and others, and the subsequent tightening of controls. More than ever, executives like to have an audit trail for their decision-making process and to know that investments are not being made on a whim or out of cronyism. Salespeople who provide a structured approach, from discovery to recommendation, are welcome standouts.

Listened Before Prescribing a Solution

This goes hand in hand with "understood my business goals." A few well-selected questions, then a willing ear, make for some of the best sales calls you will ever participate in. Let the executive talk! A sales director in Finland believes, "When you are talking, you hear only what you already know. When you are listening, you hear what you need to know!"

Salespeople who take this approach are sometimes bewildered by the results. Said one, "I really didn't do that much. I asked a few simple questions. The customer provided the answers. Then I read back a summary of what he'd said. On hearing his own words, he gave me the credit for being a great consultant with all the answers."

Doctors who get a reputation for having all the answers begin by teasing those answers out of the patient's head and letting them find expression. Most executives know what they need, especially those who have already done their homework using the Internet and other public sources of information. What they lack is time: time to reflect and time to find direction. So give them that time, and be courageous in the moments of silence. Silence is golden because it is when thoughts find their structure. Let it happen, and avoid the primal urge to fill an uncomfortable silence with your own patter.

Listening is incomplete until it is joined with *prescribing* a solution. So when you have all the executive's ideas, pain, concerns, and shopping lists on the table, this is where you add your own expertise in weaving together a debriefing on where her ideas are sound, where they could be improved, and what a working solution using your products, services, and resources would look like. The executive wants certainty, and she will buy from people who show confidence in a solution that the executive can see her own thumbprint on.

Knowledge of Industry/Company

Executives invest time with salespeople who provide insight. The best way to deliver that insight is to think of the first meeting as a job interview, as mentioned earlier, and to promote yourself as the sort of person who would make an immediate impact if the executive hired you for his team. To do this, you need to be up to date on the events of both your industry and his, and to know how his business works. You will find a guide on how to find this information in Appendix 1.

Once you have this knowledge, life becomes much easier. You can treat the first meeting and those that follow as mini–board meetings where you speak with the executive as a peer, talking not about the generic features of your product, but about the specific outcome it can drive in the business and your road map on how to get there.

Executives explained that they expect incumbent suppliers to use their knowledge of both companies to drive efficiencies. One said:

> When we bring on a supplier, we know it will take a few months for the supplier's representative to settle in and learn how we do things. After that orientation, I judge good suppliers as the ones whose representatives say things like, "We've been looking at how you do this or that around here, and we think there's a better way." When she serves as a fresh pair of eyes and uses her knowledge about my company to make suggestions nobody else has, it guarantees the longevity of the relationship. She also needs to know her own industry developments to ensure that she's giving me the most up-to-date feedback. There's nothing less valuable than yesterday's newspaper.

"Knowledge of industry/company" ranked highest of all criteria in our China study. Why is this the most important trait to China's executives? It has to do with the unique evolution of China since its 2001 entry into the World Trade Organization.

Western countries saw their infrastructures, technology, pop culture, brands, and business processes evolve in stages over the past 30 years. We all moved at a similar pace as some ways of working died out and new ones took their place. For example, 30 years ago, it was common for companies to have a typing pool of secretaries, bulky steel typewriters, messy carbon ribbons, and central filing of each original. Whole paper-based industries and brands rose up to support this way of working. Today, executives type their own e-mails, and so the secretarial typing pool, typewriters, and carbon ribbons are all but gone in the West. This shift to personal production drove a work culture of greater personal empowerment to get things done.

But in China, the typing pools of secretaries and central filing of carefully stamped or "chopped" triplicates are still commonplace alongside modern laser printers and blade servers. As in some science-fiction tale, three decades of technology and business process overlap in the same space-time continuum. It's not unusual to experience massive confusion—and therefore slow decision making—as Chinese executives face a cornucopia of bewildering options, all of them touted as the "latest and greatest." These executives admit that they don't always know whether they're investing in something new or in something that the West dispensed with 15 years ago—to them, it *all* looks new.

In such a situation, we can better appreciate why they so highly rate the ability of a salesperson (or the salesperson's manager) to bring knowledge of the industry to help them make sense of their many options and reduce the risk of losing face as a result of a wrong decision. Is this really so different from the needs of Western executives?

Ability to Solve Problems

When salespeople read this criterion, they conclude that the operative word is *solve*. Those of us in sales and marketing have an obsession with *solutions*. Type the words *your* and *solutions* into Google and insert any word in between, and you will quickly see that solutions exist for everything you need in life:

- Birth solutions
- Education solutions
- Dating solutions
- Wedding solutions
- Pregnancy solutions
- Parenting solutions
- Career solutions
- Real estate solutions
- Wealth solutions
- Vacation solutions
- Retirement solutions

And in a recent walk through New York City, the number of taxi-cabs advertising everything from toenail solutions and credit solutions to hair solutions and get-rich-quick solutions couldn't be counted. The world has gone solution-crazy, affixing the word to situations that have nothing to do with problems at all. People say *solution* when they mean *product*. So many salespeople now wax lyrical about the *synergy* of their *value-added, collaborative, enterprisewide world-class solution* that such words have become meaningless.

With all this white noise, what is a real solution? The word *solution* originates in the discipline of chemistry, where a solution is described as "a mixture comprising one or more solutes that are dissolved by a solvent of greater volume." A packet of Kool-Aid crystals (the solute) makes a refreshing beverage when the crystals are dissolved in a greater volume of water (the solvent). When your client has a defined business problem (the solute), your job is to dissolve it by application of your product or service (the solvent). This is the proper application of terms like *solve* and *solution*—they are meaningless outside of the context of a problem.

This is why the focus in the phrase "ability to solve problems" is not on the word *solve* but on the word *problem*. Without a problem, there can be no solution. Executives told us that the criteria "understood my business goals," "listened before prescribing," and "knowledge of industry/company" are all essential if salespeople are to gain a comprehensive picture of the executive's world and its unique challenges and problems. Only then do executives believe that a salesperson has the "ability to solve problems."

Tips for understanding the executive's problems were given in the first two chapters of this book. Appendix 1 provides other ideas that you can immediately apply.

Communicated Value

People at the operations level are focused on "What does your product do?" (features, functions, and their application).

People in middle management are more interested in "How will it fit into the operation?" (nonproduct issues such as total cost of ownership, implementation, training, and the impact on other processes).

At the executive level, the question changes to "Why should we do this at all?" Executives know that a dollar spent in one area is a dollar that cannot be spent in another area. So they want to know, "Do we spend $5 million on upgrading our information systems, or do we invest $5 million in a new manufacturing plant in Eastern Europe? Should we invest it in a new ad campaign, or should we build our staff an indoor squash court?" Sometimes your biggest competitor can actually be the alternative way in which a customer's capital can be spent and the competing priorities to do so.

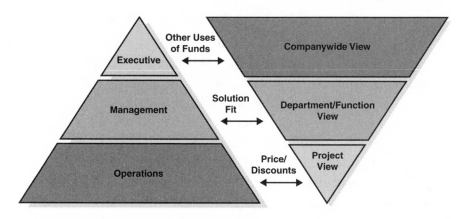

Figure 5.5 Different Stakeholders' Perspectives

As Figure 5.5 illustrates, the importance of communicating value at the executive level is that from the executive's vantage point, he has a companywide mandate to effect change, and he can tap into funds across the company to carry out his goals. When you sell to executives, the time it takes to go from spiel to deal is often shorter, but you must frame all your discussion around why this project is the right horse to back, and what the value of doing so will be.

Executives in China gave this issue of communicating value the third highest rating, compared to a rank of sixth in the U.S. studies. In China, the subtext is, "How will this decision make me look? Can I leverage it for greater *guanxi*?" Chinese executives test to know whether the salesperson can become an extension of their personal network and bring them value.

Chapter Summary

Let's summarize what we've discussed in this chapter about the third question in our research: "How can salespeople establish credibility with executives?" Let's break it down to the top three messages:

1. *Know their expectations.*

   Executives expect the salespeople they deal with to exhibit general qualities that make them stand out in a sea of look-alikes. They expect you to be able to understand their business goals, marshal your company's resources, be responsive to the executive's requests, and be accountable when things go wrong. They also expect you to listen before you prescribe a solution, to do so in the context of the executive's company and industry, to solve problems when they arise, and to return to communicate the value delivered. Beyond these general expectations are the specific expectations for the project they engage you for. But clearly their priority is on you as a person. As one executive told us: "Get people with the right values and behaviors on the team and business will work itself out."

2. *Exceed their expectations.*

   Executives feel that suppliers generally don't deliver what they say they will. They are unimpressed by salespeople who pitch canned rhetoric that fails to connect with their issues. They don't need talking brochures, and the word *solution* is applied in all the wrong places. They use a first meeting to filter salespeople who had the ability to get through the door from salespeople who will be invited back again. Salespeople who show the right capabilities gain credibility and continued access. You get only one chance to make a first good impression.

3. *Operate in the Client Value Zone.*

People buy from people they like, and they are always looking for Emerging Resources to begin to make a contribution to their organization. People also buy from people they trust, and they are always looking for Problem Solvers to clearly make a difference. At the lowest level, Commodity Suppliers are those who simply turn up to make a sale, and these almost never rate a meeting with an executive. At the highest level, Trusted Advisors are those who build trust and demonstrate their capability in equal measure. They move past the rest and become part of the executive's circle of advisors. This is what you need to aim at if your goal is to consistently sell at the executive level.

Chapter 6

How to Create Value at the Executive Level

Executives believe that meetings are a forum for exchanging ideas, and they are prepared to be led by a skilled questioner along a path of discovery in the hope that the salesperson knows what he needs to find out from the executive in order to make appropriate recommendations. Salespeople who ask the right questions to uncover problems impress senior executives.

Salespeople with experience selling to operations and middle management personnel must therefore modify their approach at the executive level. Those who give a boilerplate presentation on why their product is the best are unlikely to make progress. A number of executives told us that they feel that these canned speeches mean, "The salesperson has a pitch she wants to deliver rather than listening to my concerns." Others said: "There are a lot of salespeople who say they have the answer before they know what the problem is."

One executive said: "If I have to ask the questions or uncover all the problems, the rep is of no use to me. I look for people who ask layers of questions that uncover something I might not have considered." Note the term *layers of questions*. Executives don't want us to ask questions that merely skim the surface on the way to our product pitch. They expect a meaningful, deliberate interview that digs deep into the well of their discontent until they have unburdened themselves, arrived at the root causes, and have the potential cures before them. Salespeople who follow a structured questioning framework to bring a new perspective to an existing situation will always provide value.

This means that the majority of the meeting should be spent on understanding the problems, issues, and implications associated with the opportunity or situation. The key is to listen, ask questions, and let the executive reveal the problems and the impact that these problems are having on the organization.

STRUCTURING MEETINGS WITH THE EXECUTIVE

There is a template in Appendix 2 that you can use to help you structure your face-to-face meetings with executives to discuss their needs.

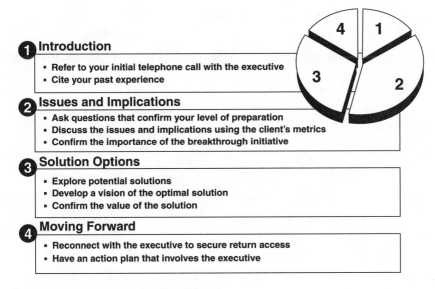

Figure 6.1 Structuring the First Meeting

Structuring an initial meeting with executives follows the same format as the pie chart in Figure 6.1, which suggests that your meeting should have an *introduction*, followed by a discussion of *issues and implications*, then deal with *solution options*, and end with *moving forward*.

The pie chart in Figure 6.1 also suggests the relative amount of time that executives told us they feel should be devoted to each part of the meeting.

For example, if the pie chart were for a one-hour meeting, the introduction might take 10 minutes, issues and implications might take 25 minutes, solution options might take 15 minutes, and agreeing on the steps for moving forward might take another 10 minutes.

1. Introduction

In the introduction stage of the meeting, you should refer to the initial phone call you made to the executive, citing your sponsor or referrer if appropriate. Give the executive a glimpse of some of your past experience, either in his organization or with similar clients. Set an expectation for the mutual value you expect the meeting to deliver. Meetings without a stated outcome are usually a waste of an executive's time.

2. Issues and Implications

This is the area you'll spend most of your time on during the first meeting. Ask questions that get you credit for having done your homework. Listen intently, and discuss the client's key business issues, using his metrics. Develop an understanding of this executive's breakthrough initiative and its importance at a personal and company level. It's a good idea to leave questions related to solution options for later in the call. Once you move to those questions, it's often hard for both you and the client to step back to the broader, more strategic questions. Try these:

- "What effect has this problem[1] had on your organization?" Use the knowledge gained from your research to expand on the situation. This question helps the executive focus on a specific area of the business and allows you to showcase your knowledge of the organization and its industry.
- "What three things are you not doing today that would help you resolve the problem?" This question helps you understand the gap between what the company is currently doing and what the executive feels it should be doing.
- "What have you done to address this problem? Why did you choose this solution? What was the outcome?" These questions all focus on using the past to understand the executive's thought process.
- "What do you see as the critical success factors for solving this problem?" This question uncovers whether the executive knows what she wants to do and gives clues about how she will measure the success of the project.

- "What are the consequences if you don't solve the problem?" This question uncovers whether this problem or situation has a compelling event that will cause pain if it is not solved within a certain time frame. If the situation has no compelling event, then pursuing a solution might not be worth the time and resources it will require.
- "Who are the key people I should talk to in your organization to better understand the problem?" With this question, you're volunteering to be sent down to lower levels in the organization to develop a better understanding of the next steps, thus allowing the executive to view you as a resource.

3. Solution Options

Only *after* the issue has been clearly defined and agreed upon should a salesperson begin to describe potential solutions that can be related to business value. Waiting until the end of the meeting to explore solutions builds credibility with the executive. Keep your product in your pocket until it's time to bring it out.

Discuss potential solutions and their value to both the company at a business level *and* the executive at a personal level. Develop the executive's vision of the optimal solution. What ideas has he already entertained? Watch for the executive's passion as he describes this vision! Don't necessarily reveal *your* company's solution at this point.

4. Moving Forward

Find a way to get the executive involved in a follow-on meeting to explore these issues in more detail. For the later meeting, you would plan to return with an expert such as a solution manager or some other presales resource to take the discussion to the next level. The executive might send you down to meet with a lower-level executive. This is not always a bad thing if you ask her to make the introduction for you, and if she agrees to reconnect with you after that meeting to review your findings. Being able to legitimately say, "The boss sent me," is like having a skeleton key that will open most doors.

Executives told us that they don't appreciate salespeople who script their meeting agenda so tightly that there's no room for creative discussion. This occurs when the rep is given a one-hour meeting block and packs enough slides to fill the whole hour. In such a setting, 20 minutes or less of presentation and 40 minutes or more of discussion is a better ratio. At its most ridiculous, we've seen this dogmatic approach lead to the executive saying, "I'm convinced; where do I sign?" and the salesperson selling beyond the close with words to the effect: "Let me just explain the benefits." Don't laugh—you'd be surprised how often we see this. Whatever sales school these salespeople went to, they learned a prescriptive approach that doesn't fit the C-suite.

As we outlined earlier, product-focused Commodity Suppliers are living in a world that doesn't really exist anymore. As a technically oriented Emerging Resource, you're living dangerously close to that old world. As a value-driven Problem Solver or Trusted Advisor who is prepared to have a robust discussion, you're at home in the new world of selling.

There was once a printing company that was expanding its business to include production of its own line of greeting cards, which it intended to distribute through retail outlets, a market the company had never sold through before.

The executive in charge asked all potential suppliers to bring him ideas on the most efficient ways to procure paper and cards for what the company anticipated would be a business with seasonal peaks.

One supplier presented several innovative suggestions about just-in-time delivery and even provided a helpful market assessment of other greeting card businesses that included the most popular card stock, sizes, and designs. The executive wanted to buy from this supplier, but his budget was not high enough, and with regret he gave a $500,000 order to a Commodity Supplier whose prices had been assessed over the Internet as being the best for cash flow.

After sending the purchase order, the paper executive called the sales manager at the winning vendor and asked whether the salesperson would receive a commission on the sale.

"Of course," was the reply.

"How much?" asked the client.

"Fifteen percent of the total sale" was the eventual answer.

The executive did some mental arithmetic. "Good," he said to the client. "Then I want my invoice reduced by $75,000 because your salesperson sold us nothing at all."

He won his concession, and he diverted the savings into a bonus for the salesperson from the other supplier who had contributed so many good ideas!

If you're a Problem Solver to your client, you see the client as a business peer because you view her business through the same lens as the relevant executive, not through the lens of a salesperson looking for a need to sell to. By researching the business using the tools we've discussed, preparing the approach, building support with influential stakeholders, and asking high-yield questions, every salesperson can sell effectively at the executive level.

Let's now discuss the concept of the value propositions we must all eventually present to our executive buyers.

GOING ONCE, TWICE, THREE TIMES—SOLD!

In the life cycle of a client, there are three times when you should sell your value.

1. Value Hypothesis

When you're on the outside hoping to gain an audience and make your first sale into an account, you should use your research to determine whether the account can *probably* derive some benefit from what you sell. You don't really know for sure. And without a discussion in which the customer validates your assumptions and provides real data, all you have is a *value hypothesis,* a guess and a hope of things that might be. Like a coloring book page, you can see an outline, but it holds no tone or definition. Value hypotheses are what marketing departments send out when they're troubling a customer about his problems—a glimpse of a desired future state.

2. Value Proposition

When you're talking to a qualified prospect and she's explaining the *how much, how often,* and *who to* aspects of the problems she faces (or the opportunities she wants to leverage), you are getting closer to knowing what the basis of your *value proposition* is going to be. It's impossible to write a value proposition unless you know what to propose, and to get at this information, you must convince the prospect to disclose something about how her business operates, where the dysfunction and costs reside, and what her vision is for an alternative. You then map your capabilities onto her requirements, and return to the prospect with a specific plan that proposes a way for her to solve her problem or achieve her vision by using your capabilities. A good proposition will always include measurements that explain:

> You want to do Z, which we can deliver at a cost of Y. This will reduce current costs by X and improve efficiency by W, which over the space of V months with U people using it, will enable you to recoup your initial cost within T months and lift overall productivity by S, adding R to your bottom line in the first year. We have these capabilities, and we propose that if you start next month, we can have this process underway as fast as Q. By doing this, Department A will solve Issue B, which is of concern to Executive C. Stakeholder group D will also benefit by having

better access to E and F, saving G amounts of time that it can better devote to the task of H. By announcing this approach in your next press meeting, your CFO expects to lift your share price by J percent, which will raise your borrowing status to AAA and open up sources of capital to underwrite your expansion plans in country K.

What you see in this alphabet soup is a value proposition that goes to the extent of naming specific people doing specific tasks, identifying how each will benefit, and determining the downstream impact on issues that you know are under discussion and are topical at the executive level. With this style of content, you're really *proposing* something. You're making an offer and packaging it in a compelling way.

The word *proposition* has a dictionary definition as follows:

An idea, offer, or plan put forward for consideration or discussion; a statement of opinion or judgment; a statement or theorem to be demonstrated.[2]

Executives told us that while millions of proposals are sent around the world each year, few of them actually *propose* anything. Don't get us wrong—most of these documents include a section dutifully titled "Value Proposition." But that's where the similarities to an actual proposition often end. There are few examples executives could recall where they sat back, rubbed their chin, and said, "Wow, I really love what these guys are proposing!" Instead of striking gold, they find their pans full of iron pyrite—fool's gold—as they read page after page of price lists and capability statements at the basic end of the spectrum, and overly detailed spreadsheets at the complex end. In few cases do they see anything that *tells a personalized story* with the names of their key stakeholders and the jobs they do, the challenges they face, and the goals they own, described against an overview of how each of these tasks and goals will be affected by a new solution. And yet, this is what executives want to see presented to them. They want suppliers to be specific and say, "This is how you do it today, this is why that isn't optimal, and we propose that if you do it our way, you'll get a specific result that looks like this."

The reason executives see winning value propositions like this all too rarely is because so many salespeople experience performance anxiety in the C-suite; they don't relax enough, or they are so intent on getting their message across that they forget to ask the very questions they need the answers to if they are to be in a position to frame a value proposition later. In the absence of customer input, all a salesperson can present or write is the chaff that is putting executives to sleep.

When you are writing a winning value proposition, it pays to connect your customer's needs with the full range of your capabilities. Salespeople sometimes overlook some of their capabilities, and so those capabilities go unannounced and unappreciated.

For example, part of your value might be that you are able to bring some of the following elements to the table, in the knowledge that they are relevant to the customer:

- Products (proprietary or custom)
- Services and support capabilities
- The stability of your company as a supplier
- Knowledge of the problem
- Familiarity with the client's environment
- Your knowledge of what works and what doesn't
- Rapport with the client's people
- Expertise in solving this problem for others
- Specialist resources in your solution team
- Introductions to others in your network
- The value of business partners in making a solution complete
- The time you will save the client

- The costs (not just the price) you will save the client
- The added capability you will provide

Don't sell yourself short. There are always many elements of value that, as you sell every day, may have become things that you regard as self-evident and somewhat pedestrian to talk about. But to a customer who is buying your solutions intermittently or for the first time, what you see as commonplace may be a revelation.

If you don't spell it out for your customer, nobody will. As one sales director once said: "If you don't blow your own horn, your competition will use it as a spittoon!"

Just remember: value is relevant only when it is explained in the context of its impact on specific problems or projects that a client has. If your value is not anchored in the client's problems, it will sound like a hustle.

A value proposition answers three questions:

1. *What's important to the client?* Simply stated, a value proposition addresses the client's issues and focuses on a return on investment for his breakthrough initiative.
2. *How does our solution create value for the client?* Address this question by describing how *you, your company,* and *your solution* can help in both a qualitative and a quantitative way.
3. *How can we demonstrate our capability?* At the nexus between your solution and the client's breakthrough initiative is a working hypothesis of *your specific business value* in terms of how tasks will be performed using your solution and how outputs will be different (see Figure 6.2). Paint a vivid picture of this specific business value.

We've established that you can construct a meaningful value proposition only if you have an understanding of the following:

- The customer's business initiative
- How your solution affects the business initiative

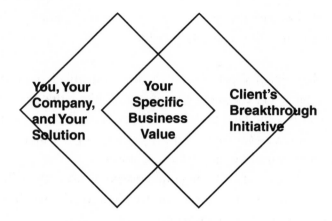

Figure 6.2 The Value Nexus

- What the customer's critical measurements are before your solution
- What the customer's measurements will be after your solution is in place
- The time frame for breakeven and ROI

Let's say that your customer is experiencing problems with her service department. It currently has an interactive voice response telephone system that processes requests from customers whose equipment has broken down.

Customers lodge their requests for repair, spare parts, or service via the phone, and these requests are automatically routed to a fleet of service vans using a global positioning system, based on which operator is closest to the customer.

Recently, some jobs have been sent to more than one van, causing two or sometimes three service representatives to arrive for the same job. This diverts them from other work that could be billed, and is a waste of time for everyone.

In this case, a good introduction to the value proposition would include a reference to this situation, as seen in Figure 6.3.

> When your service vans are dispatched to customer sites, more than one van is sent to the same site on average 30 times per month per person across a service team of 150 people. This costs your service representatives 30 minutes on each occasion and, according to your CFO, $20,000 per year in extra fuel costs. We calculate the combined cost of fuel, unproductive time, and missed revenue from this problem is $850,000 per year.

Figure 6.3 Sample Value Proposition (Introduction)

Now that you have the customer's "before" picture set, you are ready to explain the "after" picture. Figure 6.4 shows a sample value proposition for this example; a copy of the template used to prepare it is provided in Appendix 2.

For simple sales situations, this single use of the template may be all you need. However, for sales that involve multiple people, numerous departments, and varied manifestations of business pain, you should apply this format separately for each set of stakeholders or aspect of the project, then compile them all into one powerful narrative that

> You will be able to *reduce repeat customer service calls* by *20%*, resulting in a *monthly savings of $250,000*, by implementing our *Call Tracker system*. This will require an investment of *$2 million*, which will be returned in 8 months. We implemented a similar solution at *Acme Transfer Company*, which began achieving a monthly savings of *$500,000 within 90 days* of installation.

Figure 6.4 Sample Value Proposition (Main Body)

explains the full breadth of what your solution means to the prospect. Some sellers also like to provide tables and graphs that demonstrate when the client's investment will reach the breakeven point and the total return on investment over time.

A quick and easy way to experiment with this concept is to talk to a client that you recently sold to and ask her to help you fill in the blanks. Here's a step-by-step guide for doing this:

- Review the roles that are upstream and downstream from the department that bought your solution and are affected by it.
- Agree how long it takes the client to perform key tasks today, the quality or volume of that production, or whatever other metrics apply to the problems the client is trying to remedy.
- Establish the improvements anticipated from your solution. Try to attach a dollar figure to improved production, improved quality, or time saved.
- Then review the quality of the information you've gathered and compare it to the way you write value propositions today.

If you see the potential to elevate your game, adopt this approach for every new sale you get involved in. You will then be giving executives the information about value in the format they want it in, and you will sell more as a result.

3. Value Statement

The third time you talk to the client about value is after he's purchased your solution and you're now his account manager. This is when it's time to audit what you've done for your client and quantify a *value statement*. Like a quarterly frequent flyer statement, this shows all the points you've helped the client accrue as a result of his mileage with you. Remember how executives told us that they value salespeople who are willing to be accountable? This is where the rubber hits the road.

Arriving at real numbers for a value statement requires some detective work. This is why it's so important that you quantify the numbers when you describe the initial value proposition—if you don't quantify the client's pain before you install a solution, nobody will remember those numbers by the time you get around to calculating the value you delivered and describing it in a value statement.

A value statement is best delivered to the relevant executive and other key stakeholders, and is framed along the following lines:

You wanted to do Z, which we budgeted at a cost of $1 million, but it actually cost 10 percent more in out-of-scope work that nobody anticipated. We discounted that extra work by 20 percent, saving you $20,000. Within four months of starting, 100 people were using our solution and enjoying time savings and increased productivity. They tell us that you recouped your initial cost two months faster than the eight months anticipated, adding $350,000 to your bottom line in the first year. Since we've been working with Department A, we helped solve Issue B for Executive C, and we identified two other projects for additional value that have helped your factory ship 1,000 products in the same time it used to take to ship 500 products. This has added $2.7 million directly to your top line and grown your market share by 3 percent. Since you announced this approach in your press meetings, analysts lifted your share price, and your improved borrowing status has saved you $750,000 in interest and allowed you to add 20 channels in country D, which your CFO reports will add $6 million in sales this year. Our solutions represent an investment of $1,080,000, from which you have reaped gross revenues of $9.8 million, an ROI of nine dollars for every one invested with us. Now here are our ideas for building on this next year . . .

A well-written value statement is a powerful arrow, but one that our studies suggest most salespeople never remove from their quiver.

One reason they don't is that a delivery team often assumes responsibility for account management, with the salesperson remaining in a hunter role. When no obvious account manager is assigned, it's highly recommended that *someone* be appointed to read through the sales documentation that helped win the deal and look for a measurement of the problem or opportunity behind the customer's breakthrough initiative. Being able to quantify this is the starting point for calculating a statement of the value delivered.

Another reason that a value statement might not be presented is that the delivery team and/or the account manager fails to keep in contact with the key stakeholders. It's a common lament of customers that their rep comes calling only when she smells a deal brewing. Clearly, a value statement is not a tool used by transactional Commodity Suppliers.

But if you aspire to become a Trusted Advisor so that you can leverage past sales into future sales, going back over old ground and digging out the details is worth its weight in gold—or oil. There are numerous tales of entrepreneurs buying what were considered to be the worthless tailings of a gold mine that was long since spent. By carefully digging through areas known to be productive in the past, they find nuggets that evaded detection on the first pass. For example, look at the unexpected boom experienced in Alberta, Canada, when people found that they could extract oil from the dirt of old oilfields—called oil sands—which some analysts estimate hold oil equivalent to eight times the reserves in Saudi Arabia.[3]

A well-crafted value statement will help you mine a deeper well of executive credibility, possibly gaining a great customer testimonial and a renewed right to pitch your next *value hypothesis* for new business, which in turn can lead to discoveries of remarkable revenue growth.

Chapter Summary

Let's summarize what we've discussed in this chapter about the fourth question in our research: "How do you create value at the executive level?" Let's break it down to the top three messages:

1. *Plan your meetings.*
   Too many sales calls are planned in the parking lot five minutes before a meeting. You can't afford to bluff your way through an executive sales call. Structure the call so that it has a clear and compelling *introduction*. Be prepared to discuss the homework you've done on the executive's *issues* and the *implications* for his business and for him personally. Have an opinion about the *solution options* available from your company, and show your accountability and credibility for making things happen. Plan in advance what you want to get out of the meeting and what suggestions you want to extend to the executive for *moving forward*. Executives like to be asked to take action and feel that meetings are a waste of their time if they don't produce a definitive outcome.
2. *Explore cause and effect.*
   Your questioning strategy needs to focus on understanding the executive's issues and the implications if her vision is not met. You need to measure the depth, severity, and immediacy of those issues, and to gauge the executive's will to make a change. Ask who first identified the need for change, and what happened to make exploring this need a priority over other issues. Use your knowledge of the customer's business and your own product or service to

identify whether the client is focused on the root cause or just on one of the ways it manifests. Is she dealing with the real issues, or is she merely putting a finger in the dike? You will add significant value to her thought process by mapping the cause and effect, the things that are critical to get right versus the "nice to haves," the stakeholders who need a voice in the final solution, and how well the ideas she's already entertained will actually be equal to the need. This is an opportunity for you to reengineer the scope of projects and be seen as a thought leader.

3. *Sell your value three times.*

Given that you've done your homework on the executive's company and the drivers affecting it, at the start of a sale you should have a *value hypothesis* suggesting that you have value to contribute. But you don't know for sure that you have value until you can bounce the issues around with the executive and his key stakeholders. After spending time with them, you should know enough about how the business is run now and how your solution will change things to form a *value proposition*. Ask for the business, then be accountable for returning to measure the impact, and close the loop with the executive by presenting your *value statement*. Doing so will earn you credibility and may prime the pump for your next sales opportunity.

Chapter 7

Cultivating Loyalty
at the C-Suite

Client loyalty can be achieved only if relationships are consistently built and nurtured. People at the three levels of an organization (operations, middle management, and executive) have different perspectives on you, your company, and your company's solutions.

As was pointed out in Chapter 5, "How to Establish Credibility at the Executive Level," people at the operations level focus on getting the lowest price and the steepest discounts. They also want to hear the technical details of your solution so that they can compare you with your competitors and select the lowest price. Nowhere in the conversation is there any mention of value or loyalty.

At the middle management level of the organization, people want to understand how your solution can be integrated into their organization. But while their questions will be broader in nature than those posed at the operations level, they still don't focus on value and loyalty.

It's only at the executive level of the organization that the focus is on value and that loyalty can be cultivated. Executives understand how value is created and delivered, and they fully understand the true value of loyalty. Loyal relationships are important at the executive level—and most executives are open to the cultivation of those types of relationships.

In his book *The Loyalty Effect: The Hidden Force behind Growth, Profits and Lasting Value* (Boston: Harvard Business Press, 2001), Bain & Co. director Frederick F. Reichheld uses examples from State Farm and Toyota/Lexus to illustrate that loyal clients lead to substantial profitability over the long term.

According to Reichheld:

> One common barrier to better loyalty and higher productivity is the fact that a lot of business executives, and virtually all accounting departments, treat income and outlays as if they occurred in separate worlds. The truth is, revenues and costs are inextricably linked, and decisions that focus on one or the other—as opposed to both—often misfire.

Companies cannot succeed or grow unless they can serve their customers with a better value proposition than the competition. Measuring customer and employee loyalty can accurately gauge the weaknesses in a company's value proposition and help to prescribe a cure.

While every loyalty leader's strategy is unique, all of them build on the following eight elements:

1. Building a superior customer value proposition
2. Finding the right customers
3. Earning customer loyalty
4. Finding the right employees
5. Earning employee loyalty
6. Gaining cost advantage through superior productivity
7. Finding the right [capital sources] and
8. Earning [their] loyalty.

Reichheld found that those clients who give greater loyalty typically generate more profit over the lifetime of their patronage. We agree. Increased profitability from customer retention occurs because:

- Acquisition costs are incurred only at the beginning, and are amortized over the life of the relationship.
- Long-term customers provide annuities and are less sensitive to annual price increases, within reason.
- As trust is developed, referrals follow.
- Purchases of add-on products and upgrades are a natural extension over time.
- Regular customers require less education, and repeat exposure allows the seller to build expertise with each client.

But as our own research consistently found, typically there is a gap between the value you deliver and what the executives think you delivered. In Chapter 5, "How to Establish Credibility at the Executive

Level," we observed that this could happen because, although the supplier has done an outstanding job, nobody bothers to tell the executive about it!

Having coached the world's largest companies, it never fails to surprise us how businesses that are so smart in most things can be so cavalier in how they look after their customer relationship management. There's a certain lemminglike behavior we see, with companies calling their salespeople "account managers" without giving much thought to what "account" and "manager" really mean. When these companies weight the sales commissions and bonuses of account managers to favor the pursuit and capture of new customers, the account managers adopt a sell-and-run mentality. By default, the customer relationship is transferred to the delivery team, whose members are usually technically proficient, but lacking in sales and service acumen.

Everybody thinks that the customer is being "account managed" because the account manager's job title suggests it. But the way the account managers are rewarded drives hunter behavior and is at odds with the mandate implied in the job title. At the end of the day, you get the behavior that you measure and reward. When customers vote with their feet, it is often to the complete astonishment of the members of the vendor's management team, who seldom recognize that their own dysfunction caused the migration and routinely slash their prices as an incentive to win the customer back.

Client executives report a strong attraction for the companies that recruit a different breed of person to farm the account (hunters and farmers are entirely different breeds, as any psychometric profile will immediately demonstrate), and then remunerate them for displaying appropriate behavior, then track and communicate the value delivered. They also indicate a higher interest in remaining loyal if the recent positive experiences remain consistent over time.

If the recent experience exceeds expectations, customer loyalty is likely to be high. Loyalty can also be high even with poor performance if the expectations were originally set low; if switching costs are high; if there are no alternatives; if the social, cultural, or ethnic relationship is not easily replaced; or if there are other lock-ins such as contractual terms, shared technology, economic codependence, or a geographical imperative to retain the same suppliers even though they do only an average job.

As shown earlier in this book, senior executives typically get involved in the buying cycle for major decisions at two specific times: early in the buying process to set the overall project strategy, and late in the buying cycle to measure the results and understand the value that the solution provider has delivered to them and their company.

At the second point at which they get involved, senior executives in the client organization look to the salesperson to provide them with regular input on the value that the solution provider has created and delivered to their organization. By providing that information, the salesperson is in a position to clearly describe and communicate value—value that she can differentiate from that provided by her competitors and use to develop loyalty.

That sense of loyalty is best achieved at the executive level because this is where you can obtain the best leverage. Senior executives have a companywide view of the organization and will typically ask questions that are focused on value and the return on investment of your solution, whereas lower-level executives may be focused only on price and discounts.

In his book *PowerSkills: Building Top Level Relationships for Bottom-Line Results* (Nimbus Press, 2000), James Masciarelli talks about the competitive advantage of cultivating loyal customers:

> [Today], more than ever, capital and products appear to be far less important for developing a sustainable competitive advantage than cultivating loyal customers and employees.

STEPS IN CULTIVATING CLIENT LOYALTY

Cultivating client loyalty is a methodical process that often combines the business and personal aspects of relationships with client executives. Most salespeople focus solely on expanding the business relationship and ignore the personal side of the relationship. Often, asking executives probing questions can quickly determine areas of common interest that can lead to lasting relationships.

By finding out what is important to the executive, you may get a glimpse of his personal agenda—and if you can address both his personal and his business agendas, you have an opportunity to connect business solutions to his personal motivations, and deliver value from both a business and a personal perspective.

For example, if a client executive's personal agenda is to secure a key promotion within the company, finding a business solution to one of his critical business objectives may satisfy both his personal and his business needs. You will have then scored a major victory and created the basis for a lasting relationship.

So how do you pull this off?

It's like climbing the steps of a staircase—*a Loyalty Staircase*—where simple actions on the lower steps provide a foundation for ascending to the next step until you reach the top (see Figure 7.1). This is a tried and tested approach used by the world's most successful salespeople,

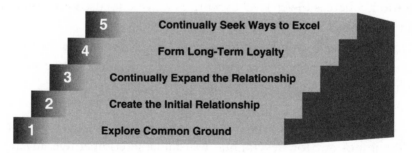

Figure 7.1 The Loyalty Staircase

and, importantly, it is validated by the executives themselves as what they reward salespeople for doing.

Now let's go climbing . . .

Step 1. Explore Common Ground

Client executives expect you to know what's important to them—so make certain that you do your homework before your initial meeting with them. In today's Internet age, that task has been made significantly easier. There are a myriad of Web sites you can access to obtain information about your client, but here are a few ideas, some of which have little to do with using the Internet!

- Go to the client's Web site and access the last few annual reports. Within each annual report, pay special attention to the "President's Letter to Shareholders." This document contains a treasure trove of information about the key business and industry drivers, along with some of the initiatives that the company has put in place to address those drivers. Most salespeople focus on trying to dissect the annual report and drill down on the company's financials (which are important); however, the President's Letter offers a much better perspective on some of the company's important (and immediate) business issues.

- Access business, financial, and industry sites that allow you to compare how this company stacks up against its competitors in the same industry. You'll be able to see how your client compares with other companies in the same industry with respect to profitability, growth, and other important business metrics. Some of those sites are listed in Appendix 1 of this book, "Guide to Customer Research."

- Another important perspective about your client can be obtained from its quarterly earnings conference calls to financial analysts. While not all companies conduct this type of call, those that do offer yet another opportunity for insight and analysis.

Typically, information about the quarterly earnings call will be found on the company Web site, which will give both the day and time of the call and the person responsible for conducting it. This individual will usually be the CEO, the president, or the chief financial officer. The call will typically cover the following types of information:

- Results from the previous quarter
- Outlook for future results
- Questions from financial analysts

As noted earlier, this call can also offer insightful information about the problems and the key business issues facing the company and its plans to address some of those issues.

The company's marketing department will often have profiles of the company's key executives, as well as recent speeches those executives have delivered. Some of this information may also be available on the Internet; however, by accessing the marketing department, you may receive additional insight and background regarding those executives and what they have been saying publicly.

Focus on the interests of each executive you contact, and if, during the relationship, you find something that you think might be of value to her, send it to her by e-mail or some other method. This lets the executive know that you're thinking about her, something that doesn't necessarily have to be achieved through a face-to-face meeting. Explore common ground by seeing how the executive's problems, goals, and initiatives fit with your solutions and capabilities. Look for ways to demonstrate competence in areas that are important to the client and in which you have a track record of success.

Step 2. Create the Initial Relationship

Look for ways to create an initial positive experience to begin the relationship with the client. Make certain that your solution will create and deliver value to the client and that you have a comprehensive implementation plan that exceeds the client's expectations. If possible, offer not only your best solution but alternatives that could also deliver value to the client. This is particularly true in the initial phase of your relationship with the client. Whatever you offer the client in this initial phase, you should do everything possible to make certain that it's as flawless as it can be. Remember, you never have a second chance to make a first good impression—and this is especially important when you're beginning a relationship with a new client.

Overcommunicating at this stage of the relationship is often better, as long as your communications are concise, relevant, and timely. This may be your first opportunity to communicate with the client executive on a business level, and you want the executive to see how you operate at that level. However, make certain that you're not perceived as a sycophant. Your objective is to keep the executive updated on the key issues and obstacles you have faced and how you resolved them—not simply to please the executive so as to gain personal advantage.

Step 3. Continually Expand the Relationship

Find ways to learn more about your client's business and continually expand your relationships with additional executives in the client organization. Here's where you have to take the relationship up a notch. This could involve working with lower-level executives to gain a better understanding of the client's business, or conducting advanced searches on the Internet to gain a better understanding of the key industry trends that your client is facing. Working with lower-level people in the client organization can pay substantial dividends if the executive refers you to those people (especially if he provides an introduction for you). The executive has indicated his confidence in the person to whom he referred you, and that person now understands the importance of meeting with you. Make certain you exploit both sides of that internal relationship.

Once you are committed to an expanded level of relationship with the executive, you should always be trying to expand the scope of the overall client relationship to include other key executives in the organization. You never know where the next opportunity for your solution may lie—it could be in a different functional area, in another part of the country, in another part of the world, or even in another company if the executive changes companies at some point in the future. Your reputation for delivering value is what you are seeking to enhance and expand.

Always be sure to exceed expectations in all areas—large and small—and to honor your commitments, no matter how small they may seem. Simply returning phone calls on a timely basis and going the extra mile when you respond to the executive's questions can go a long way toward increasing the executive's perception that you always conduct yourself in a businesslike manner.

Always listen to your client's issues and problems before you propose any solution. Make certain that you are seen as always adding value—from your personal perspective, using your company's resources and offering your company's solutions that create value. If necessary, offer partner resources when you don't have a complete solution. And lastly, make certain that you clearly and consistently communicate the value of your solutions—never assume that the executive fully understands the value that you deliver. In fact, consider conducting an annual meeting with selected client executives specifically to communicate the value you have delivered during that year and your expectations for the coming year.

Step 4. Form Long-Term Loyalty

Long-term loyalty is the result of your continuous commitment to excellence in every task. When your client faces difficulties, make certain that you stand by her—particularly if the adversity was (in any way) caused by your solution. Make yourself present and available when she is going through difficult times, offering your support whenever possible. Accept responsibility for any mistakes that you (or your company or partners) made, and resolve them as quickly as possible. Executives understand that mistakes can happen—it's how people respond to them that counts (in their eyes). In forming long-term loyalty, as when the client comes to perceive you as a Trusted Advisor, the relationship often becomes collaborative. Senior executives then begin to look for ways to demonstrate that they acknowledge that level of relationship with you.

Here's an example of how one senior executive demonstrated that her relationship with the salesperson was a collaborative one:

A salesperson sold a series of training workshops to a major client and developed what he thought was a Trusted Advisor relationship with a senior client executive at the firm. During the fourth quarter of the year, the client executive informed the salesperson that she would not be conducting any additional workshops until the first quarter of the next year because of budget constraints.

The salesperson indicated that he had some prospects who were interested in personally observing a training workshop—the exact type of workshop that had been delivered at this client's location.

As a quid pro quo for the value delivered by this salesperson, the client executive agreed to conduct one additional workshop during the fourth quarter so that the salesperson's prospects could observe the session, as this would help the salesperson close additional business.

It was obvious that the salesperson's relationship with that client executive had become collaborative—a direct result of client loyalty developed over the long term.

Step 5. Continually Seek Ways to Excel

As you continue to enhance the client relationship, you have multiple opportunities to add value to the client organization and, perhaps more importantly, to the client executive as well. You will progress from subject matter expert to Trusted Advisor and beyond, where you can easily come to be perceived as a consultant to the client executive. A key way for you to measure your progress in this area is by analyzing the questions the client executive poses to you. When the executive starts asking you questions about her business that are totally unrelated to your company's products and services, you know that you have achieved that status.

It's easy to be visible to clients when there are no problems at the client's installation site. But what happens when things go wrong— what should you do? Do you pretend that you're working behind the scenes to try to solve the problem, or do you make yourself visible to the client executive, showing him that you understand his pain and that you're trying to deliver value by helping to solve the problem?

Make certain that you're visible to the client when things aren't going well. He will reward you for it.

Here's a story that illustrates how the salesperson's presence and availability during difficult times can demonstrate value to the client:

A mainframe computer that a salesperson had recently sold to her largest manufacturing client was down for nearly a week. That computer had quickly become an integral part of the company's business: scheduling the plant floor, ordering the right parts and supplies, and controlling the inventory. Now it had been out of service for nearly four days!

It was very unusual for a mainframe from this vendor to experience this amount of excessive downtime. However, the salesperson made certain that she brought all her service resources to bear to solve the problem. She scheduled an appointment with the client executive and brought the service branch manager with her so that she could show the client that she was attempting to deliver value and help solve the issue. She made certain that she had the right regional service specialists addressing the problem, and she even had engineers fly in from the company's manufacturing plant. The mainframe was repaired, and the client's manufacturing plant was back in operation.

During that entire time, the salesperson made certain that she was visible to all the key client executives of the firm—and it certainly paid large dividends for her in the years that followed. The client never forgot that she was there when things went wrong.

That's when the executive told her: "You show up when things go wrong, not just when they go right!" He also told her how much he appreciated her visibility during that time, and it helped her to solidify her position as his Trusted Advisor.

Cultivating client loyalty through executive selling can clearly be achieved by consciously implementing a step-by-step process that begins with exploring common ground with the executive and culminates in a long-term loyal relationship. While carrying out this process will take some time, always remember which step you are currently on so that you can optimize your position. Beyond that, you should constantly seek ways to excel—to continually differentiate the value you deliver to the client organization—so that the relationship can be sustained and expanded even if there are changes at the executive level.

That is also why you should expand your relationships to other executives in the client organization. Never be satisfied with having a Trusted Advisor relationship with a single key executive or with having cultivated a loyal relationship with a single executive. Executives move to different firms, retire, or take on second careers. It's important that you continually expand your cultivation of loyalty to other executives in the client organization. Also, by creating loyal relationships with additional executives, you expand your network, and you are then in a position to optimize those relationships—whether in the same organization or in other organizations as executives migrate to other firms.

When those executives do migrate to other firms, even if those firms are in different industries, they may seek your guidance regarding similar solutions. Executives tend to have long memories of those who have created and delivered value for them—and they will always reward those salespeople who have demonstrated loyalty to them. You'll then be in a situation where you can begin the relationship at the top of the Loyalty Staircase!

Chapter Summary

Let's summarize the top three messages in this chapter:

1. *Value drives loyalty.*

   Don't let your experiences with transaction-focused subordinates lead you into thinking that executives share their buying culture. While the buying culture of some companies emanates from the top, most executives told us that they are open to the idea of loyalty in the buyer-seller relationship. The currency you exchange for their loyalty is the consistent delivery of value. Like beauty, value is in the eye of the beholder, so you need to know what each executive considers valuable, consistently deliver that level of value, and make sure you get credit for your good work. If your contribution is not recognized, it holds no value for you.

2. *Climb the Loyalty Staircase.*

   Almost anybody can sell to an executive once, at the bottom step of a staircase. Enjoying repeated success in the C-suite requires doing things well on a consistent basis, one step at a time. Remember to treat executives with respect, but treat them like everyday people, too. Don't fear them, and don't pander to them. Explore common ground and demonstrate what you know. You can never be guilty of overcommunication when your intent is to make a genuine contribution. It's critical that you and the members of your team focus on excellence. Nothing should be too much trouble. Demonstrate that your attitude is to serve and to make a difference. When problems occur, be the first to identify and rectify them.

Show yourself as being proactive and "on the ball." As you do these things, you will be invited into the executive's circle, you will meet more of the people he confides in, and you will develop loyalty.

3. *Quantify the value.*

Use the executive's industry and company metrics to explain the value you will deliver. Wherever possible, quantify the value in terms of time saved, problems eliminated, risk reduced, revenue increased, or costs removed. Give evidence of where and how you have done this before, the time frame required, and the projected return on investment and breakeven point. Consider asking your company's financial staff to help you prepare and present complex financial information. As stated previously, after you deliver the value, make sure that you turn your good work into customer loyalty to prime the next deal.

Afterword

SELLING TO THE C-SUITE

In today's competitive environment, as professional salespeople strive to differentiate themselves and retain established clients, they need to constantly seek to reach higher levels in the client's organization and build long-term relationships. Selling at the executive level requires a different set of skills and strategies from selling at the more traditional departmental level or making transactional sales.

In this book, we have tried to outline some simple strategies for creating, maintaining, and leveraging relationships with senior-level executives in your client organizations. While that sounds simple, many salespeople continue to be reluctant to call on senior-level client executives.

Let's review some of the challenges professional salespeople have in calling on senior client executives. Typically, when we pose this question to a group of professional salespeople, we tell them that we know that none of *them* have challenges in calling on client executives—so we ask them to tell us about the challenges they think some of their friends might have in calling on executives!

Interviews with thousands of top salespeople confirm the following types of challenges:

- Recognizing the importance of the *relevant* executive in the current sales campaign
- Selecting the right executive to call on
- Identifying the right approach to use in accessing the executive
- Determining the best time in the client's buying cycle to meet with the executive
- Getting past the gatekeeper
- Having an in-depth understanding of the executive's key business issues
- Being intimidated by the questions that might arise during the meeting
- Jeopardizing lower-level relationships

We can summarize those challenges as three simple issues, all of which can be addressed by the actions described in this book. Those three issues are:

- Inability to identify the relevant executive
- Lack of self-confidence and fear of failure in calling on executives
- Being blocked from getting to the relevant executive

Simply put, the actions you can take to mitigate those challenges can be summarized as thorough preparation, constant practice, and determination, combined with a degree of perseverance. Thorough preparation means that you have done your homework prior to your first encounter with a client executive, and that you have a fairly good understanding of the executive's key business issues and how your company's solutions might create value, both for that executive and for the executive's company. Through practice and determination in calling on executives at that level, you will increase your self-confidence and overcome your fear of failure. The preparation you did in advance of your meeting with the executive will also decrease the possibility of your being intimated by the questions that an executive might pose.

Remember that each and every salesperson has had to make that initial call on a key client executive for the very first time—and that's true no matter how many sales calls a professional salesperson has made in his lifetime. And lastly, through perseverance, you will be able to navigate the political structures of the client organization to the point where you'll be a master not only of circumventing gatekeepers but also of pleasing key players in the organization by calling on and interfacing with the right people.

SIX CRITICAL STEPS IN CREATING, MAINTAINING, AND LEVERAGING RELATIONSHIPS WITH CLIENT EXECUTIVES

1. *Identify the relevant executive.* This entire process starts with identifying the relevant executive for the sales opportunity. Remember that we defined the relevant executive as the executive who stands to gain the most or lose the most as a result of the application or project associated with the sales opportunity. It's critical that you identify the relevant executive early in the sales cycle, so that you can maintain your focus on that key executive.

2. *Determine the best approach to get to the relevant executive.* Once a salesperson has identified the relevant executive, obtaining a meeting with that executive is typically not very difficult. Feedback from executives we surveyed indicates that they are most likely to grant a meeting to a salesperson if the request for that meeting comes from a credible source within their own organization. In fact, in the first two studies conducted, 84 percent of the executives interviewed said that they would usually or always grant a meeting if the salesperson was recommended internally. However, the most

important factor in that process is that the recommendation must come from someone whom the executive deems to be credible. If the executive does not deem the salesperson's sponsor within the client organization to be credible, the salesperson's chance of getting a meeting with the executive is considerably reduced. According to our studies, other methods of access were clearly less effective. Referrals from people outside the organization would yield a meeting approximately 50 percent of the time; however, cold calls to the executive (even those following a letter or an e-mail) worked only about 20 percent of the time.

3. *Perform the appropriate research before that critical first meeting with an executive.* Not having an in-depth understanding of the executive's key business issues could represent the single biggest stumbling block for a salesperson who's about to meet with a client executive for the first time. Executives have little or no tolerance for salespeople who have not done their homework prior to a key meeting with them. In the surveys we conducted, C-level leaders stated in very clear language that they expect the people who meet with them to have an in-depth understanding of the key business issues facing them and to listen intently before proposing any product or service solutions.

   Developing in-depth learning about the client is the fastest way to be in a position to contribute insight and create long-term collaborative relationships with senior-level client executives. As we demonstrated, client learning occurs on three levels—the client's industry, the client's company, and then, lastly, the client executive herself—and at each level you become more valuable to the client executive. Remember, Appendix 1 to this book is a "Guide to Customer Research."

4. *Conduct an effective first meeting with the client executive.* Throughout this book, we've stressed the importance of that critical initial face-to-face meeting with a client executive. In fact, we even gave you a template for conducting that meeting

(see Figure 6.1). In any case, you need to remember that you never have a second chance to make a first good impression!

Your objective for that critical first meeting is to begin to create a lasting relationship with the client executive. To that end, your focus should not be on a short-term product sale, but on a longer-term relationship that transcends any short-term sales.

5. *Demonstrate integrity and capability in subsequent meetings, so that the executive perceives you as a Trusted Advisor.* When client executives perceive that you have demonstrated that you are reliable and trustworthy on a consistent basis, you will have achieved a level of personal integrity with them. In addition, when client executives perceive that you have demonstrated both insight and expertise, they will begin to recognize that you have a level of capability that, combined with your level of integrity, can lead to a collaborative relationship. When this happens, you will be operating in the Client Value Zone and ultimately come to be perceived as a Trusted Advisor by the client executive.

   It is important to point out, however, that this level of business relationship may not be achievable with all clients. Some clients may not want this level of relationship, and you also have to understand the extent of your involvement—in terms of both time and resources—in developing a Trusted Advisor type of relationship. It may be that with some clients, this level of relationship is simply not worth the required investment. As the manager of your sales territory, you have to make that decision.

6. *Consistently communicate your value to the executive.* Don't overlook opportunities to communicate the value of your solution to the client executive. The CXO-level executives we meet continually say that they like to get involved at the end of the buying cycle to understand the value that a salesperson's solution has delivered to them.

In Figure 6.2 we clearly outlined the fact that your value has three components: the value you bring to the client's company, the value your company's resources bring to the client, and the value your solution brings to the client's company. Make certain that you take advantage of the opportunity to communicate those three components of value, particularly following the installation of your solution. As a salesperson, you may want to implement a formal process that ensures some level of consistent communication with client executives to review the specific value that your company delivers to them.

For example, some vendors explain to their customers that to ensure that promises are fulfilled and expectations are managed, an annual client account review meeting should be scheduled on the anniversary of signing the first contract. These meetings focus on reporting to *all* relevant executives the specific changes that have occurred in the customer's business as a result of your solution's being installed. Account managers take special care to review with each stakeholder the reasons for needing a solution that he gave during the sales cycle, and his expectations for what the right solution would do for him personally, for others working in the same department, and across the business overall. With this information tucked away, you can then revisit the customer three, six, or twelve months after the deal was closed and the solution installed to measure the extent to which those original expectations are being delivered.

If expectations *are not* being met, this meeting provides an opportunity to explore the reasons why and resolve the problems; this demonstrates accountability and the ability to marshal resources (two traits that executives say they look for in their suppliers).

If expectations *are* being met *or exceeded*, the client account review is an opportunity to get credit for your good work from each stakeholder who influenced the decision. This helps prime the pump for the next opportunity, and is a key to loyalty, as discussed previously.

A FINAL WORD

Calling on senior-level client executives can be compared to learning to play golf. It takes time, effort, and a high level of energy to become proficient. Calling at the executive level is a learned skill; it's not something you're born with, and, like golf, it usually improves only with a lot of constant practice. The more times you make a certain type of shot in golf or make a key call at the executive level, the more proficient and, perhaps even more important, the more comfortable you become. You'll spend many hours practicing your skill of calling at the executive level, and after some of those experiences, you may get frustrated and feel that the efforts you have expended have not been worth it. Even the most seasoned professionals on the PGA Tour blow a shot now and then. But take it from the authors of this book, who have more than 60 years of combined sales experience in calling on executives: *there's nothing like the thrill of closing a big deal—especially when it comes with the help of that Trusted C-suite Advisor in the client organization who was working behind the scenes to help close the deal!*

Do these things well, and you are on your way to mastering selling to the C-suite.

Good luck with the journey!

Guide to Customer Research

LEARNING ABOUT YOUR CLIENTS

There are three levels of research involved in learning about your client: research on the industry, the company, and the executive himself (see Figure A1.1). Knowing about your client at these key levels will help you formulate an incisive and meaningful value proposition.

To get your research rolling, here are some key pointers and Internet resources that should quickly guide you to the information you need.

Information on Your Client's Industry

Most executives expect sales professionals to have a certain degree of industry knowledge and expertise. You have to be conversant with the issues, pressures, and trends in your client's industry so that you can create the most value for your client.

We recommend www.business.com.

This site is described as

> "The leading business search engine and directory designed to help its users find the companies, products, services, and information they need to make the right business decisions [*offering*] the Internet's only business-focused search engine and directory."

Figure A1.1 Three Levels of Client Research

Another fee-based site for industry profiles is www.firstresearch .com.

This site provides reasonably priced, in-depth industry analysis and market research on virtually every industry.

Information on Your Client's Company

Your ability to suggest new ideas and strategies increases dramatically as you become more knowledgeable about your client's strategy and operations.

We recommend: www.bizlink.org.

The mission of the Bizlink Web site is *"to support the local, national, and international business communities and others conducting business research. Bizlink provides access to selected electronic and print business resources."*

Research links include a focus on Canadian-based companies and includes:

- Company research
- Industry research
- International business
- Investment and personal finance
- Marketing and demographics

Client Executive Knowledge

This may be the most important area to research. There are several ways to obtain information about individual executives, such as using a search engine to find the executive's name accompanied by words such as *strategy, announce,* or *press release* and the current year. Adding *.pdf* and *.ppt* to your search may unearth presentations to investors or other Webinars that your prospect or client company posted on the Web and forgot to take down; these can often be downloaded and reveal the goals and issues that the executive has gone on record as supporting. Such information is golden!

We recommend the following:

Brint	www.brint.com
CEO Go	www.CEOgo.com
Dialogweb	www.dialogweb.com
Dow Jones News	www.dowjones.com
Dun & Bradstreet	www.dnb.com
Executive Library	www.executivelibrary.com
Faulkner Information	www.faulkner.com
Hoover's	www.hoovers.com
Lexis-Nexis	www.lexis-nexis.com
One Source	www.onesource.com

INTERNET BROWSERS AND SEARCH ENGINES

The Internet has truly revolutionized the way we access and retrieve information. It provides the ability to research client organizations at the three levels quickly and efficiently:

- The client's industry
- The client's company
- The client executive

You are probably already familiar with browsers such as Internet Explorer, Safari, and Firefox. Some of this content assumes a basic level of proficiency with browsers.

A *search engine* is a program that is typically accessed as a Web site (e.g., www.google.com) and that allows you to search for information by typing key words, phrases, or questions into a search field. Most sites offer "Advanced Search" or similarly named options that can increase the effectiveness of your searches. Power users can learn how to incorporate special "operators" into their searches to target the desired information more accurately.

See www.google.com/help/refinesearch.html for an excellent guide to using operators and other advanced techniques.

There are many search engines to choose from. Here are a few of the most popular:

AltaVista	www.altavista.com
Google	www.google.com
Hotbot	www.hotbot.com
Internet Address Finder	www.iaf.net
Lycos	www.lycos.com
MetaCrawler	www.metacrawler.com
Search	www.search.com
Webcrawler	www.webcrawler.com
Yahoo!	www.yahoo.com

BUSINESS PERIODICALS AND NEWS SERVICES

The following sites offer substantial amounts of information on company news. Browse them and bookmark the ones that are most relevant to you:

Associated Press	www.ap.org
BusinessWeek	www.businessweek.com
Computerworld	www.computerworld.com
Fast Company	www.fastcompany.com
Forbes	www.forbes.com
Fortune	www.fortune.com
Gartner	www.gartner.com
Harvard Business Review	www.harvardbusiness.org
McKinsey Quarterly	www.mckinseyquarterly.com
News Link	www.newslink.org

PR Newswire	www.prnewswire.com
Reuters News Agency	www.reuters.com
Sales and Marketing	
Management	www.salesandmarketing.com
Selling Power	www.sellingpower.com
The Economist	www.economist.com
The Red Herring	www.redherring.com
Wall Street Journal	www.wsj.com

PREPARING FOR THE INITIAL FACE-TO-FACE CALL ON A CLIENT EXECUTIVE

Now that you understand that you have to conduct research on your client's industry, your client's company, and the client executive, you'll want to start consolidating that information so that you can conduct an intelligent first conversation with a client executive.

The worksheet at the end of this appendix helps you capture the type of information that you'd typically want to have at your fingertips prior to that first critical conversation with the client. This will enable you to be perceived by the client executive as a thought leader who's both professional and prepared. In addition, you can use this information to develop key questions to pose to the client executive.

Remember, it's better to first show the executive that you've done some homework on the company and its industry, then use that information to probe for the executive's insights on those areas—information that you typically can't retrieve from a public source like the Internet. This will show the executive that you are honoring his time by doing the appropriate homework and being prepared for the initial conversation.

Examples of Questions You Should Answer Prior to Your Initial Face-to-Face Call on a Client Executive

What are the most recent trends in the client's industry?

_____

_____

_____

_____

What is the client's position within the industry? How do this client's metrics compare with those of the industry leaders?

_____

_____

_____

_____

What are the client's goals or mission?

_____

_____

_____

_____

What are the client's key business drivers and initiatives? What is the client's breakthrough initiative, and what is compelling the client to change?

_____

_____

_____

_____

What payback will the client achieve if this initiative is implemented, or what consequences will the client suffer as a result of not implementing this initiative?

_____

_____

_____

_____

What questions will you ask the client executive on your initial call?

_____

_____

_____

_____

What additional key points do you want to make on your first call on the executive (to get credit for having done your homework)?

_____

_____

_____

_____

What solution(s) can you offer the client that will affect the breakthrough initiative?

_____

_____

_____

_____

Tools for Building the Executive Relationship

SALES OPPORTUNITY PROFILE

SALESPERSON	CLIENT

SALES OPPORTUNITY	EXPECTED REVENUE

Describe the client's application or project.

What is the basis for your pursuit of this opportunity?

Outline your solution that will enable you to effectively compete
for this opportunity.

Can you win this opportunity by calling on executives with whom
you've already established a relationship? If NO, with whom else will you need
to establish a relationship?

Who is the relevant executive for this sales opportunity?

How will you access that executive?

INITIAL EXECUTIVE TELEPHONE CALL PLANNER

Introduction

- Provide a brief introduction of you and your company.
- Explain your connection to the person who referred you to the executive, if appropriate.

Purpose

Be clear, concise, and specific as you explain the reason you are contacting the executive.

Credibility

Explain the homework you've done on the organization and communicate how you've helped other companies address similar challenges.

Commitment to Action

Propose a clear and specific action for the executive to take.

ROADBLOCK WORKSHEET

Which executive are you attempting to access?

Why does the roadblock exist?

What are the risks associated with attempting to gain access
to the relevant executive?

What are the risks (short-term and long-term) of not getting
to the relevant executive in this sales campaign?

What will you do?

BUSINESS ISSUES WORKSHEET

Drivers
What are the internal or external factors that might cause the client to change or react?

Two Internal Factors	
Financial	Operational

Six External Factors	
Customers	Competitors
Suppliers	Business Partners
Regulatory Issues	Globalization

Breakthrough Initiative
What is the most important initiative the client must act upon? It is typically bound by a time frame and accompanied by significant payback or consequences.

Issues Impacting the Breakthrough Initiative

Your Solution
• How does your solution address the breakthrough initiative and provide payback? • How can you differentiate the value of your solution?

EXECUTIVE-LEVEL MEETING PLANNER

Introduction

- Refer to your initial telephone call with the executive.
- Cite your past experience.

Issues and Implications

- Ask questions that confirm your level of preparation.
- Discuss the issues and implications.
- Confirm the impor-tance of the break-through initiative.

Solution Options

- Explore potential solutions.
- Develop a vision of the optimal solution.
- Confirm the value of the solution.

Moving Forward

- Reconnect with the executive to secure return access.
- Create an action plan that involves the executive.

VALUE PROPOSITION WORKSHEET

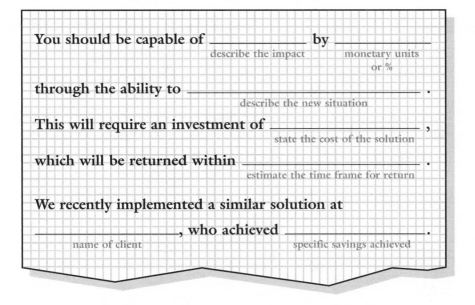

You should be capable of _____ by _____
                              describe the impact   monetary units
                                                           or %

through the ability to _____.
                             describe the new situation

This will require an investment of _____,
                                state the cost of the solution

which will be returned within _____.
                             estimate the time frame for return

We recently implemented a similar solution at
_____, who achieved _____.
name of client   specific savings achieved

Create Your Specific Value Proposition for This Client

EXECUTIVE PRESENTATION GUIDE—PAGE 1

Company Name	Presentation Date	Account Manager Name/Phone

Name of Relevant Executive	Title and Responsibilities

Application/Project	Impact of This Project on the Relevant Executive

Describe Our Solution for This Project

Background of the Relevant Executive (Previous Jobs/Company Affiliations)	Recent Key Decisions Made

Universities Attended and Degrees Received	Affiliations with Other Company Boards

Relevant Executive's Decision Criteria for This Project

Executive's Business Agenda or Focus	Executive's Personal Agenda or Focus

Other Client Executives Expected to Participate in the Presentation		
Name	Title	Responsibilities

Additional Participants from Our Company	
Name	Phone

EXECUTIVE PRESENTATION GUIDE—PAGE 2

Key Issues That Might Arise During the Presentation

Major Competitors and the Solution(s) They May Offer

Our Relationship with the Relevant Executive

What do we think is our current level of relationship with the relevant executive?

☐ Commodity Supplier   ☐ Emerging Resource   ☐ Problem Solver   ☐ Trusted Advisor

What actions have we taken (with this client and specifically with this executive) to achieve that level of relationship?

What specific actions has the relevant executive implemented or taken to demonstrate this level of relationship?

EXECUTIVE PRESENTATION GUIDE—PAGE 3

Presenting Your Solution to the Executive

Introduction/Presentation Objectives

Outline the objectives of the presentation and confirm the overall agenda.

Issues and Implications

Describe the project or application, making certain you demonstrate a clear understanding of the key issues facing the executive.

Solution Options

Explore potential solutions and their value to both the executive and the company.

EXECUTIVE PRESENTATION GUIDE—PAGE 4

Presenting Your Solution to the Executive

Contrast the Value of Your Proposed Solution

Develop a graphical picture of the current approach and contrast it with your proposed solution to dramatically depict the differences, as well as the additional value.

Moving Forward – Suggested Next Steps

Outline the next steps, as well as your expectations for the executive's involvement in those next steps.
(This is your way of securing return access.)

EXECUTIVE PRESENTATION GUIDE—PAGE 5

- ☐ Was your presentation focused on the relevant executive and the executive's company?
  - — Did it clearly demonstrate an understanding of the executive's key business issues?
  - — Did you contrast the current approach and the approach of your proposed solution?
  - — Were the differences clear, and was the proposed solution dramatically better?
  - — Did you clearly articulate your specific business value, and did it include you and your company as well as your solution?
  - — Did you present a plan for moving forward, and did that plan clearly involve the executive in multiple steps or stages?
- ☐ Did you involve the appropriate key personnel from the client organization in developing the presentation to the relevant executive?
- ☐ Were you able to collect appropriate information about the relevant executive and thoroughly analyze it before preparing your presentation?
- ☐ Did you communicate that information to your team before the presentation to the executive?
- ☐ Prior to the presentation, did you try to assign each member of your team to a corresponding member of the client team?
- ☐ Did you rehearse your presentation and have someone give you constructive feedback and suggestions for improvement?
- ☐ Did you ask for feedback about the presentation from the relevant executive before you left the meeting?
- ☐ Did you recognize and thank the people from the client organization who helped you develop the presentation?
- ☐ Did you ask and get feedback from those same people about their reaction to the presentation?
- ☐ Do you have a plan to reconnect with the relevant executive in a timely fashion to keep the momentum of the project moving forward?

Notes

Chapter 1

1 John A. Byrne, "How Jack Welch Runs GE," *BusinessWeek*, June 8, 1998.

2 Geoffrey A. Moore, *Inside the Tornado: Strategies for Developing, Leveraging, and Surviving Hypergrowth Markets* (New York: Collins, 1995).

3 Everett M. Rogers, "New Product Adoption and Diffusion," *Journal of Consumer Research* 2 (March 1976), pp. 290–301. See also http://en. wikipedia.org/wiki/Everett_Rogers.

4 Years after this deal, NBC won the right to broadcast *Sunday Night Football* and ESPN won *Monday Night Football*. The tug-of-war between rival salespeople for the same account is a constant in almost all industries.

5 Sally Jenkins, "Peacock Power," *Sports Illustrated*, December 25, 1995. See also http://sportsillustrated.cnn.com/events/1996/olympics/story-olympic/nbc.html.

Chapter 2

1 Interview with Neil Rackham by Josh Krist, a content manager for SalesLobby, a sales resource Web site operated by the Alexander Group Inc., September 2000.

See also http://www.saleslobby.com/OnlineMagazine/0900/features_ NRackham.asp.

2 www.eloqua.com.

3 www.v-trenz.com.

Chapter 3

1 *Journal of Air Transport Management* 10, no. 1 (January 2004).

2 "Global CEO Turnover Rises," Weber Shandwick, March 3, 2008.

3 Matthew Kirdahy, "CEO Turnover Increased in 2007," *Forbes*, March 7, 2008.

4 Booz Allen Hamilton, "CEO Succession 2006," *Strategy + Business*, issue 47 (2007).

5 "Fortune 100 CEO's Average Tenure," *Executive Recruiter News*, May 1, 2007.

Chapter 4

1 United Nations press release SG/SM/6161, February 19, 1997.

2 Joshua Green, "Karl Rove in a Corner," *Atlantic Monthly*, November 2004.

3 James Moore and Wayne Slater, *Bush's Brain: How Karl Rove Made George W. Bush Presidential,*" (New York: John Wiley & Sons, 2003).

4 Hannah Beech, "Wretched Excess," *Time*, September 2002.

Chapter 6

1 You can substitute other words for the word *problem* as required, such as *situation, project, opportunity, breakthrough initiative,* or the specific business driver that's at the heart of the discussion.

2 encarta.msn.com/dictionary_/proposition.html.

3 "The Oil Sands of Alberta," *60 Minutes*, CBS. Originally aired January 22, 2006.

Recommended Associations

You need a license to drive a car or an aircraft, a certificate to fix pipes or wires, and a degree to practice engineering or law. Yet there is no formal accreditation for the profession of selling, despite the fact that it plays a mission-critical role in business.

Selling requires its practitioners to be responsible for projecting complex financial calculations worthy of any accountant; for high-stakes negotiations worthy of any statesman; for designing elegant solutions worthy of any architect; for delivering presentations worthy of any advertising director; for exercising competitive savvy worthy of any strategist; for demonstrating leadership under pressure worthy of any general; for preserving customer confidences worthy of any priest; for helping customers find their own answers worthy of any psychologist; for packaging visual and narrative information worthy of any producer; for educating customers worthy of any teacher.

We could go on, but you get the point. Selling is many roles rolled into one. Yet educational institutions have largely ignored the profession. It would be polite to say that the universities don't know how to classify such a diverse role. But the truth is that most of them simply don't see sales as a profession with standards and disciplines that can be taught and measured. If marketing is criticized as being the domain of *breakfasts and brochures*, sales is known for *lunches and lattes*. It took until 2002 for such stereotypes to be overcome and for standards to be drafted for teaching professional selling at the university level.

University Sales Center Alliance

Formed in 2002, the University Sales Center Alliance (USCA) is an organization that helps universities promote selling to students as a viable career option by sharing information on how to establish the academic stream and then assisting in the sharing of best practices for curriculum development, intercollegiate sales competitions, placement of graduates, and other related consulting activities. Its Web site lists universities that teach Sales as a degree program.

www.salescenteralliance.com/.

National Collegiate Sales Competition

The National Collegiate Sales Competition (NCSC) was launched to promote the sales profession as an attractive career choice by providing a forum where students enrolled in a certified sales degree program could compete and exhibit their skills against national rival schools, and providing corporate sponsors with an opportunity to preview students for their recruitment pool. Its Web site also lists universities that teach sales as a degree program.

www.coles.kennesaw.edu/ncsc/.

PROFESSIONAL SOCIETY FOR SALES AND MARKETING TRAINING

Since 1940, the Professional Society for Sales and Marketing Training (SMT) has offered publications, conferences, and best practices on sales, marketing, and management to corporate training practitioners and sales professionals. Membership in SMT is a prerequisite for universities entering the University Sales Center Alliance.

www.smt.org/.

Strategic Account Management Association

Founded in 1964, the Strategic Account Management Association (SAMA) is devoted to advancing the professional development of individuals and companies involved in managing national, global, and strategic customer relationships. SAMA also runs U.S.-based, pan-European, and pan-Asian conferences each year.

www.strategicaccounts.org/.

In addition to the universities and professional associations listed here, we are pleased to see the addition of Sales and Customer Service as a field of recognition in the annual international business awards.

The Stevie Awards for Sales & Customer Service

The Stevie Awards (from *stephen*, the Greek word for "crowned") is a global business awards competition created to honor and generate public recognition of the achievements of organizations and businesspeople worldwide. Beginning with the American Business Awards in 2002, followed by the International Business Awards in 2003, the Stevie Awards for Women in Business in 2004, and now the Stevie Awards for Sales & Customer Service since 2006, the mission of the judging panel is to raise the profile of exemplary companies and individuals among the press, the business community, and the general public. Dubbed "the business world's own Oscars" by the *New York Post*, the 24-karat gold and crystal Stevie Award was designed by R. S. Owens, the same company that makes the Oscar, Emmy, and Clio Awards.

We encourage salespeople everywhere to make use of these and other resources for this most challenging and rewarding of professions.

Recommended Reading

Go into any physical or online bookstore and you'll find thousands of books related to sales, marketing, management strategy, and so forth. Some of them are better than others. The following have helped us on our journey.

On Selling

Action Selling, by Duane Sparks. Minneapolis: The Sales Board Inc., 2004.

Clients for Life: How Great Professionals Develop Breakthrough Relationships, by Jagdish Sheth and Andrew Sobel. New York: Simon & Schuster, 2000.

From Vendor to Business Resource, by Jerry Stapleton. Fort Collins, Colo.: Summa Business Books, 2002.

Get-Real Selling, by Michael Bowland and Keith Hawk. Nova Vista Publishing, 2008.

How Winners Sell, by Dave Stein. Austin, Tex.: Bard Press, 2002.

Managing with Power: Politics and Influence in Organizations, by Jeffrey Pfeffer. Boston: Harvard Business School Press, 1994.

Persuasive Business Proposals, by Tom Sant. New York: AMACOM, 2003.

Power and Influence: Beyond Formal Authority, by John P. Kotter. New York: Free Press, 1985.

The Relationship Advantage—Become a Trusted Advisor and Create Clients for Life, by Tom Stevenson and Sam Barcus. Chicago: Dearborn Trade Publishing, 2003.

Rethinking the Sales Force: Redefining Selling to Create and Capture Customer Value, by Neil Rackham and John Devincentis. New York: McGraw-Hill, 1999.

SPIN Selling, by Neil Rackham. New York: McGraw-Hill, 1988.

The Trusted Advisor, by David H. Maister, Charles H. Green, and Robert M. Galford. New York: Free Press, 2000.

On Marketing

The Anatomy of Buzz: How to Create Word of Mouth Marketing, by Emanuel Rosen. New York: Doubleday Business, 2002.

The Buck Starts Here: Profit-Based Sales & Marketing Made Easy, by Mary A. Molloy and Michael K. Molloy. Cincinnati, Ohio: Thomson Executive Press, 1996.

Crossing the Chasm: Marketing and Selling Technology Products to Mainstream Customers, by Geoffrey A. Moore. New York: HarperCollins, 1991.

Escaping the Black Hole: Minimizing the Damage from the Marketing-Sales Disconnect, by Robert J. Schmonsees. Mason, Ohio: Southwestern Educational Publishing, 2005.

Inside the Tornado: Strategies for Developing, Leveraging, and Surviving Hypergrowth Markets, by Geoffrey A. Moore. New York: Collins Business, 2004.

The Leaky Funnel, 2nd ed., by Hugh Macfarlane. South Melbourne, MathMarketing, 2007.

Sell the Brand First: How to Sell Your Brand and Create Lasting Customer Loyalty, by Dan Stiff. New York: McGraw-Hill, 2006.

The Tipping Point: How Little Things Can Make a Big Difference, by Malcolm Gladwell. Boston: Little, Brown, 2000.

On Personal Professionalism

Awaken the Giant Within, by Anthony Robbins. New York: Free Press, 1992.

The 4-Hour Work Week, by Timothy Ferriss. New York: Crown Publishers, 2007.

How to Win Friends and Influence People, by Dale Carnegie. New York: Pocket Books, 1988.

The 7 Habits of Highly Effective People, by Stephen R. Covey. New York: Free Press, 2004.

True Professionalism, by David H. Maister. New York: Free Press, 1997.

On Western Strategy

The Art of War for Executives: Ancient Knowledge for Today's Business Professional, by Donald G. Krause. New York: Perigee, 2007.

On War, by Baron Carl von Clausewitz. New York: Oxford University Press, 2007.

The Prince, by Niccolò Machiavelli. New York: Bantam Classics, 1984.

The U.S. Army/Marine Corps Counterinsurgency Field Manual, with an introduction by General David H. Petraeus, Lt. General James F. Amos, and Lt. Colonel John A. Nagl. Chicago: University of Chicago Press, 2007.

On Eastern Strategy

The Art of War, by Sun Tzu, with a foreword by James Clavell. New York: Delta, 1989.

The Book of Five Rings, by Miyamoto Musashi. New York: Shambhala, 2005.

China, Inc., by Ted Fishman. New York: Scribner, 2005.

Hide a Dagger Behind a Smile: Use the 36 Ancient Chinese Strategies to Seize the Competitive Edge, by Kaihan Krippendorff. Avon, Mass.: Adams Media, 2008.

Thick Face, Black Heart: The Warrior Philosophy for Conquering the Challenges of Business and Life, by Chin-Ning Chu. New York: Business Plus, 1998.

On Global Perspective

1421: The Year China Discovered America, by Gavin Menzies. New York: HarperCollins, 2003.

None Dare Call It Conspiracy, revised edition, by Gary Allen and Larry Abraham. Cutchogue, N.Y.: Buccaneer Books, 1982.

The Post-American World, by Fareed Zakaria. New York: W. W. Norton and Company, 2008.

The True Story of the Bilderberg Group, by Daniel Estulin. Waterville, Ore.: TrineDay, 2007.

Wikinomics: How Mass Collaboration Change Everything, expanded edition, by Don Tapscott and Anthony D. Williams. New York: Portfolio Hardcover, 2008.

The Wisdom of Crowds, by James Surowiecki. New York: Anchor, 2005.

The World Is Flat: A Brief History of the Twenty-First Century, by Thomas L. Friedman. New York: Farrar, Straus and Giroux, 2005.

On Sales Training

Sales Coaching: Making the Great Leap from Sales Manager to Sales Coach, by Linda Richardson. New York: McGraw-Hill, 1996.

Sales: Games and Activities for Trainers, by Gary B. Connor and John A. Woods. New York: McGraw Hill, 1997.

Sales Training Solutions, by Renie McClay. Chicago: Kaplan, 2006.

Index

About the Authors

Nicholas A. C. Read is president of the consulting firm SalesLabs, which helps companies drive predictable and repeatable revenue growth through the application of improved processes, measurement, and skills. He was previously executive director of the Revenue & Growth Risk Services practice at Ernst & Young. The author of several sales and management workshops, including the award-winning *Target Opportunity Planning*, Nic has sold on the phone, in the showroom, in the field, and on the Web, and has managed large sales teams in the IT&T, financial services, and consulting industries. He has trained business-to-business salespeople and their managers in more than 40 countries in a career spanning more than 20 years. Nic consulted on organizational change and sales and marketing alignment across Europe after the fall of the Berlin Wall, and was based in England and Germany. He followed the wave of globalization to Asia in 2002, and was based in Beijing, Shanghai, and Singapore. He and his wife are now raising four little salespeople of their own. Learn more at www.saleslabs.com.

Stephen J. Bistritz, Ed.D., spent more than 27 years with IBM in senior roles in sales training, direct sales, and sales management. He later served as vice president of development at OnTarget, Inc., for the bestselling *Target Account Selling* (TAS) and *Selling to Senior Executives* (SSE) workshops, which have been delivered to tens of thousands of professional salespeople worldwide. Steve has been published by *Marketing Management,* the *Sales & Marketing Executive Report,* and the *Journal of Selling & Major Account Management.* He is a regular contributor to annual conferences for Microsoft, the Strategic Account Management Association (SAMA), and the Professional Society for Sales and Marketing Training (SMT). Steve is the immediate past president of SMT and serves on a variety of corporate and academic advisory boards, where his practical experience makes him a leading authority in the sales profession. He holds a doctorate in human resource development from Vanderbilt University and lives in Atlanta with his wife, Claire, three grown children, and five grandchildren. He now leads his own sales training and consulting firm based in Atlanta, Georgia. Learn more at www.sellxl.com.

Don't forget to send us your success stories at **Stories@CXO-Selling.com** and we'll consider publishing them as examples in future editions of this book.